MW01027334

"J. P. Conway raises a challenging question tian community that is not always hones~~t about the pain it~~ perpetuates? Conway's response is an honest confession of the hurt the church causes, but also an unwavering hope of what the church can be when community is celebrated. He makes a compelling case that life in the church is worth it."

—CHARLES STROBEL
Founding Director, Room in the Inn

"I love remodeling houses. Tearing down walls and busting up bricks is pretty easy. Building walls back and pouring new cement is hard. In *Broken But Beautiful*, J. P. Conway reminds us that 'religious deconstruction is easy—reconstruction of the church demands sacrifice.' This book is very timely as we watch the church decline in numbers in our country."

—DUDLEY CHANCEY
Professor of Ministry, Oklahoma Christian University

"One reason I love this book is that it is full of vivid stories that tell the truth about church—true-to-life, heart-breaking, push-through-the-pain, uplifting stories. Another reason I love this book is J. P.'s winning portrayal of the intentionally intergenerational church that binds up the wounded while providing a hothouse for spiritual formation for all ages. The third reason I love this book is that it is hopeful—a book of encouragement for ministry leaders struggling in churches that are broken and reminding them that churches are also beautiful. It is simply the most winning, hopeful book about church that I've read; it is J. P. Conway's love letter to the body of Christ."

—HOLLY CATTERTON ALLEN
Co-author of *Intergenerational Christian Formation: Bringing the Whole Church Together for Ministry, Community, and Worship*

"Burnt by the church? Apathetic toward the church? Bored by the church? This book is for you. Against the background of his narrative, J. P. extends an invitation to all, to learn from the brokenness of the church, to be warmed by her beauty, and to establish her worth as life-giving for self, family, and community."

—STAN WEBER
Operation Andrew's Director of United4Hope, Nashville

"I have found *Broken but Beautiful* to be a truly beautiful book for a too often tragically broken church in today's world. J. P. honestly addresses the flaws and brokenness of the church and empathizes with those who are disappointed by and have left the church. J. P., however, calls them to come back to church by seeing the church as Jesus sees, 'beautiful' enough to give his life for."

—GARY PARRETT

Former Professor of Educational Ministries and Worship,
Gordon-Conwell Theological Seminary

Broken but Beautiful

Broken but Beautiful

Why Church Is Still Worth It

Joseph P. Conway

WIPF & STOCK · Eugene, Oregon

BROKEN BUT BEAUTIFUL
Why Church Is Still Worth It

Copyright © 2020 Joseph P. Conway. All rights reserved. Except for brief quotations
in critical publications or reviews, no part of this book may be reproduced in any
manner without prior written permission from the publisher. Write: Permissions,
Wipf and Stock Publishers, 199 W. 8th Ave., Suite 3, Eugene, OR 97401.

Wipf & Stock
An Imprint of Wipf and Stock Publishers
199 W. 8th Ave., Suite 3
Eugene, OR 97401

www.wipfandstock.com

PAPERBACK ISBN: 978-1-7252-7146-3
HARDCOVER ISBN: 978-1-7252-7145-6
EBOOK ISBN: 978-1-7252-7147-0

Manufactured in the U.S.A.   11/04/20

Scriptures taken from the Holy Bible, New International Version®, NIV®. Copyright
© 1973, 1978, 1984, 2011 by Biblica, Inc.™ Used by permission of Zondervan. All
rights reserved worldwide. www.zondervan.com The "NIV" and "New International
Version" are trademarks registered in the United States Patent and Trademark Office
by Biblica, Inc.™

To all the ordinary churches who meet in ordinary neighborhoods in ordinary buildings: you are worth it. Through the Spirit, God does extraordinary works through you every day. You are the body of Jesus, the bride of Christ. Never forget that.

Contents

Preface

Room in the Inn began in the winter of 1985, when founding director Father Charles Strobel opened the doors of his parish to individuals seeking sanctuary in the church parking lot. In December 1986, four congregations committed to sheltering people experiencing homelessness through March 1987. By the end of that winter, thirty-one congregations had joined. Now, nearly 200 congregations representing a wide variety of traditions and over 7,000 volunteers shelter almost 1,500 men and women each winter. In 1995, Room in the Inn opened their downtown campus, offering emergency services, transitional programs, and long-term solutions to help people rebuild their lives. The opening of a 45,000-square-foot facility in 2010 further enhanced their ability to support people through programs emphasizing health, education, employment, and housing. They do this work through building one-on-one relationships and offering hospitality to all who call the streets of Nashville home. Roomintheinn.org

All royalties from the sale of this work will be distributed to Room in the Inn.

Acknowledgements

OVER THE YEARS, MANY friends have honestly shared their hurt and pain, as well as their hopes and dreams. I'm thankful for your vulnerability.

I'm grateful for the churches which have nurtured me over the years, from childhood to college to my time as a minister—Una, Smith Springs, Highland, Southwest, Manchester, Smyrna, and Acklen Avenue.

I've had the honor to know so many people over the last twenty years of congregational ministry. Forgive me for the ways I fell short. I'm thankful for the time we had together. You were and continue to be the body of Christ to me.

I'm thankful for the many people who supported this project, especially in the moments when I doubted or felt overwhelmed. Specifically, Holly, Leonard, Earl, Sheila, Robbie, Spencer, Matt, Bryan, and Paul gave essential feedback and support at key times.

I'm grateful for the encouragement I receive from students and faculty at Lipscomb University, where I'm honored to serve as affiliate faculty.

My parents and brothers show up in so many of these stories. Thank you for your faithfulness at the time and your openness in letting me share a part of your lives in this work. Moreover, my life would not be the same without the support of my in-laws: mother, father, brothers, and sisters.

I'm grateful for the vibrant joy my three daughters bring to my life. I relish watching you encounter Jesus and experience the love of a church family.

To my wife, Beth, your unwavering commitment to Jesus inspires me every day. Your refusal to harbor cynicism and resentment about church life, even when it gets really hard, has been a true gift. For the countless hours we processed these ideas and stories out loud together, thank you. Gently, you provoked deeper reflection and action. I couldn't imagine a better life and ministry partner than you.

Introduction

A Broken Body

As I began my senior year in college in 1999, 70 percent of Americans held membership in a local church. Twenty years later, as I enter my forties, that number has plummeted to 50 percent.[1] I'm not surprised by these statistics. Every week, I encounter a friend or meet someone new who tells me they no longer participate in church. Most continue to identify as Christian or at the very least as spiritual. After I ask a few questions, their frustration floods out like water from a poorly designed dam. The reasons for departure stream out: feeling judged, feeling shame, the culture wars, the politics, the cover-ups and abuse, the anti-science attitude, the boredom.

We're experiencing a religious sea change in America. In 1955, 95 percent of Americans identified as Christian.[2] In surveys taken between 2014 and 2017, that number shrunk to 69 percent, the number marking "other" grew from 4 percent to 11 percent, and those marking "none" grew from 1 percent to 20 percent. The "Nones" now represent the fastest growing religious demographic in America, surpassing evangelicals (23.1 percent vs. 22.5 percent) and mainline Protestants (11.8 percent). In addition, approximately 10 percent of the American population falls under the category of "churchless Christians." They identify as Christian, but while they once attended church regularly, they haven't attended a church in six months.[3]

1. Jones, "U.S. Church Membership Down."
2. Saad, "Catholics' Church Attendance."
3. Barna Group, "Meet Those Who 'Love Jesus.'"

I live in Nashville, Tennessee, what some refer to as the "buckle" of the Bible Belt. Still, I rub elbows with "Nones" and "churchless Christians" every single day. They're not strangers but friends and neighbors. I'd like to think I understand the decisions they've made. I get it. Their concerns have a ring of legitimacy. I get why so many have left because I've thought about leaving too. When I entered congregational ministry around twenty years ago, an old minister told me, "never quit on Monday." I responded with a nervous laugh. I didn't get it. I get it now. To be sure, some Mondays, I float along on the wave of inspiration of the day before. Other Mondays, I limp around in confusion, even doubt. Is it worth it? Is too much of it broken? Why is it so hard?

Deep down, a lingering thought wouldn't go away. What if there is more than just the brokenness? Beyond the pain and difficulty, what if something beautiful endures beneath the baggage? So, ultimately, I've stayed. But if you've left, though, I want you to know that I get it. I'm sorry for the pain you've endured. I'm honored you're reading this, and I invite you on this journey. I invite you to look into the depths of the brokenness and wait for the beauty to rise. And if you haven't left, I want you to consider why you've stayed. Some of us have stayed out of guilt or shame. Some of us have stayed because it's just plain easier. But imagine what it would look like to stay, not out of guilt, but out of conviction. Imagine what it would feel like to stay, not to avoid social embarrassment, but for the beauty of it all.

I've thought about leaving, but I haven't. This is why . . .

Years ago, my buddy Chuck and I hung out a lot and were very close. When he began dating a girl, I missed his friendship a lot. But it was more than just that. I worried she wasn't right for him. I don't mean to be rude, but she had some issues. Far from healthy, she struggled to keep her head above water in the midst of physical, emotional, and spiritual challenges. I liked her, but I worried about the long-term feasibility of the relationship. I worried that he would end up getting hurt. Admittedly, this happened more than once in my twenties. Maybe you had the same experience. What do you do when a friend enters a relationship that concerns you?

At first, I tried to talk Chuck out of it. Gently but firmly, I pointed out the challenges. Careful not to disparage her, I instead focused on his capacity to walk with her through hardship. Maybe they could just be friends. Maybe he could give it a bit more time before he committed. I tried to warn him, to talk him out of it, but I failed. So, after they got serious, I changed my strategy. I tried to change her. We hung out in groups, and as the extremes of her personality surfaced, I tried to confront her. You can imagine the awkwardness that created, but I cared about my friend. When she ventured towards poor choices, I tried to point out the pitfalls to both him and her. You can imagine the strain that put on our relationship, and you can probably imagine the result. I tried to change her, but I failed.

So when my first two strategies failed, I took a resentful third option. I quit spending time with her, which meant I didn't spend much time around Chuck either. Watching their relationship frustrated me too much. Over and over, she got in over her head with financial problems, broken relationships, and work issues. Over and over, he dropped everything to go be with her. I couldn't take it, so I walked away. Eventually, they got married, and I hardly saw them. I congratulated myself on taking a firm stand, but deep down I missed Chuck. I hadn't affected anything or anyone but myself. I'd lost the relationship, so eventually, after a few years, I reached back out.

Along with my wife, the four of us all went to dinner one night. I noticed something. Sure, many alarming, self-destructive aspects of her personality remained. At the same time, I noticed some traits I'd never seen before. I noticed her patience. I noticed her kindness. I noticed her resolve. Gradually, as the evening went on, I began to see what he saw in her. She was not just broken. She was beautiful. I saw the beauty he saw in her. I had tried to talk him into walking away, but I failed. I tried to change her, but I failed. I tried to remove myself but only hurt myself. When I began to see her the way he saw her, it made all the difference. Maybe you've been there.

For many, our relationship with church proves similar. We first fell in love with Jesus, and because of Jesus we hung out with the church. But we've struggled with how to process the relationship between Jesus and the church. In Ephesians 5:25, Paul says, "Christ loved the church and gave himself up for her." Imagine this. Imagine Jesus was your buddy. Imagine that Jesus started dating a girl named the church. Now, you know the church. You've spent time with her. I mean this lovingly, but she's crazy. You never know what the church is going to do. She'll break your heart. At times, she's even guilty of evil. So, you try to talk Jesus out of it. Surely, Jesus can do life without the church. Wouldn't Jesus be healthier without this relationship? But Jesus loves her. So, you try to change her. You try to change the church, and, as expected, that fails. Frustrated and unwilling to watch the pain Jesus will no doubt endure, you walk away. You stop spending time with the church, and as a result maybe you spend less time with Jesus as well. Eventually, you wonder if you're only hurting yourself. After a long time apart, you meet back up with the church. Sure, the church still has issues, but you notice things you've never noticed before. She's still broken, and yet, she's beautiful. You begin to realize what he sees in her. And as you begin to see what he sees, it changes everything. Maybe you've been there.

Each Sunday, I meet with a very imperfect group of Christians. We meet in an ordinary brick building and conduct an ordinary service. Our worship climaxes at what we call the Lord's Table. As we prepare to eat the bread and drink the cup, I look around the room. I see people overwhelmed with life. Some older members have buried spouses and children. I see middle-aged adults trying to pay their bills, raise their kids, and sustain their marriages. I see conservatives and liberals, traditionalists and progressives, Republicans and Democrats. I see some who were born in America and some who moved to America. I see some with thriving faith and some barely holding on to faith. Some have even lost faith. I see some experiencing deep pain that only a few others know about. I see some who have been very upset with me at times. I see others who think more highly of me than they should. I see little kids crawling all over the pews. I see teenagers, some bored and some engaged. I see some single and some married, some happily married and some considering divorce. I see people struggling with various forms of addiction and anxiety. I see people wanting to make a difference, to make our neighborhood and city a little better each day.

These are my people. They have my back. This is my family gathered around the Lord's Table. In these moments, I look towards the front. A buddy holds up the bread and says, "This is the body of Christ, broken for you." It's so beautiful. And then, he breaks it. He breaks the bread because the body has been broken. We pass it around, and we all eat it. At this moment, a sensation of transcendent peace overwhelms me. A hopeful reality sets in. I get a glimpse of truth. It may be broken, but it's still beautiful. That beauty keeps me going, keeps me coming back.

For the past ten years, I've wrestled with why I've stayed. I want to share what I discovered. While some names have been changed, it's all true. This is my story.

Section 1 explores why our experience in church often seems so broken. I'll highlight the trends I find responsible for our current statistics. The fundamental issue lies in the brokenness of the human condition, clearly seen in the sinful hypocrisy of the church. Over the last fifty years in America, the awareness of sin has caused widespread distrust of institutions and communal structures, including the church. Many no longer seek out the very forms that brought community to former generations. To combat this, many embraced consumerist models to stem the tide of withdrawal in their organizations. In the American church culture, we saw this in the church growth movement, which birthed among other things the megachurch. While this stemmed the tide for some, it made it worse for others. Together, all these trends have culminated in today's loneliness epidemic. We feel disconnected, and we act in disconnected ways. In doing so, we alienate each other more and more. A certain slice of Americans has responded by continuing their pursuit of Jesus but doing it outside of organized communities of faith. However, I wonder if these churchless Christians, sisters and brothers, will find what they're looking for in the long run.

Section 2 explores why church manifests a persistent beauty despite the underlying challenges. Jesus entered a broken world and lived a beautiful life. He gave us a taste of heaven. In doing so, Jesus confirmed our deepest longing and suspicion: we were created for something more than this. This better life takes place in the kingdom, where what God wants to happen actually happens. Jesus showed us it's more than just a naïve fantasy. It's real. Of course, how do we live as kingdom residents in a world that seems anything but heaven? The Bible answers this with the theme of exile, which explains why our present experience so often differs from our ideal future. Flowing from an understanding of kingdom and exile, we begin to realize the true nature of the church, the body and bride of Christ. Combined, these metaphors show us what to pursue as well as the love we discover as we fail. Alongside this, an exploration of the Christian practices of baptism and Communion offer key tools to recapture God's intention for human flourishing.

Also in section 2, I'll walk through four unique aspects of the church. No other social institution offers these things, at least not in the same way. First, the church provides open weekly gatherings. In a culture fervently seeking inclusiveness, these accessible gatherings offer an instant and low-cost entry point for anyone who comes. Second, the church presents one of the only contexts for all ages to be together. In an era of age segregation, where else can you find babies and Baby Boomers, teenagers and Millennials, all hanging out doing life alongside one another? Third, the church, at its best, gives us a transnational identity, even a global family. We're part of something enormous made up of every tongue and tribe as Revelation 7 tells us. Fourth, the church offers a means of ethical transformation that holds us accountable to the example of Jesus. While we can all point to exceptions, as a general rule, participation in the life and rhythms of congregational life shapes one's behavior.

Section 3 explores why the broken but beautiful church is still worth it. Regular church involvement over the long run produces thick culture. In contrast to thin connections, churches produce an overlapping web of relational support. Moreover, thick culture leads to the production of social capital. People with social capital frequently say things like "I know a guy who can . . ." and call lots of people "uncle" and "aunt." From getting jobs to processing challenges to meeting tangible needs, they look socially rich, no matter their bank account. Taken together, this social wealth flows out from the church to the community and transforms our cities. Church promotes the common good. Of course, all of this is not without challenge. Yet, the challenges shape and mature us. Perhaps we should think of church as we think of going to the gym. Working out is hard, but it's supposed to be hard. The challenge of church becomes not a hardship to avoid but an opportunity for us to grow. If we give ourselves over to a lifetime of loving difficult people and seeking communal renewal, we'll grow to be more like Jesus. Finally, I'll offer reflections on how to thrive in a normal everyday church on your street. People choose churches for a variety of reasons, yet we've seen some choices produce better results than others. How can we think through that, form appropriate expectations and boundaries, and end up with a spiritual family that quenches the thirst God has given us for relationship?

If you've walked away, I get it. If you're hanging by a thread, I understand. I've been there. Your frustrations and disappointments are real. Yet, I want you to consider giving it one more chance. Jesus is the love of my life, and even though I've thought of leaving church, I've learned that I get to spend more time with Jesus when I spend time with her. Years ago, I decided to stay in ordinary, messy churches, and it's been so worth it. Through all the rough patches, I've learned to love her. She's worth it.

SECTION 1

Broken

1

Who Is My Mother?

A FEW MONTHS AFTER I turned eight, my mother passed away in a car accident. Up to this moment, I had an idyllic childhood. I grew up in in the country, on the edge of the suburbs. I knew all my neighbors. On summer days, my mother sent me outside barefooted and shirtless for a day of running and exploring in the woods. There were two simple rules. First, don't go inside, because then I wouldn't be able to hear if she called me. Second, don't climb an unfamiliar fence. Like rule one, this kept me within shouting earshot.

I built clubhouses. I shot arrows into hay bales. I helped my dad build a barn. I climbed trees. I played Pee Wee baseball. A few years ago, my wife framed a picture for me. Probably around age seven, I'm in the center of the photo clothed in my blue Royals baseball uniform. My father stands on one side as the coach. My mother stands on the other side in her "Team Mom" shirt. My brother joins us in the picture, likely as a bat-boy or helper even though he played on an older team. I keep this picture on my nightstand. I think of it as my Eden picture. It's what my life looked like before the fall.

On two summers, in 1985 and 1986, we went on month-long RV trips with my maternal grandparents. The six of us (my parents, grandparents, older brother and me) piled into the RV together. As Dad drove and Gramps held the map, my older brother and I rode in an upper compartment with a window. We had a perfect view of all that lay ahead. Sometimes, we'd sit at the kitchen table with Mom and Granny. Mom would play cards with us, and Granny would read us Louisa May Alcott books. I got to see the

Grand Canyon, Yosemite, Yellowstone, the Statue of Liberty, Niagara Falls, and the Rocky Mountains. Still, my favorite part was simply riding my bike and swimming at the little campgrounds along the way. By the end of the second trip, I'd been to over forty states. Life was perfect.

About a month later, my mother died. Our family had driven to Alabama on Labor Day weekend to visit my paternal grandfather. A young driver in the other lane swerved into our 1985 Toyota Corolla. My mother died instantly, but I didn't know it for hours. The rest of us survived, even as my father experienced serious injuries. He had to stay in Alabama for a week. My maternal grandparents came and took us back home. We stayed with church friends for a couple of days and then back at our house with my grandparents. I remember my Aunt Anna May came in from Kansas City to help out.

I'll never forget the day of the funeral, which my father missed due to his injuries. I sat there on the front row with my brother and grandparents. The church was packed. The preacher said some nice and encouraging things. I had to dress up, which wasn't my favorite thing at that age. All of my best friends came to the funeral. They didn't know what to say, which was fine because I didn't really want to talk about it. I remember the burial. I'd watch the casket being lowered, and then I'd take a break and play tag. It all felt like a fog. It was not how I thought my life would go.

Like so many others who experience tragedy, we tried to figure out how to continue on and do life one day at a time. I missed my mother dearly. But on top of that, I just felt incredibly lonely. My father and brother were rocks during that time and remain my heroes. Still, as we grieved and tried to figure out what life would be, I felt isolated and alone.

For several years, I sought language to describe my thoughts and emotions. Eventually, I found those words in an unlikely place. You may remember the romantic comedy *Sleepless in Seattle* with Tom Hanks and Meg Ryan. I know, this sounds like an unlikely place. Early in the film, a recently widowed Tom Hanks calls into a radio talk show. After sharing his loss, the therapist/host asks him, "What are you going to do?" His response: "Well, I'm gonna get out of bed every morning . . . breathe in and out all day long. Then, after a while I won't have to remind myself to get out of bed every morning and breathe in and out . . . and, then after a while, I won't have to think about how I had it great and perfect for a while." I probably saw that movie seven or eight years after my loss, and instantly I thought, "Yep, that's what it's like. That's what I went through."

Have you been there? As an adult, I now know I'm not that unique. My social worker friends refer to this as an Adverse Childhood Experience (ACE for short). So many kids experience these. Moreover, we've all experienced extreme brokenness and painful disappointments. We have all loved and lost. Regular life free of huge tragedies remains challenging and difficult. Bills, debts, tornadoes, wildfires, gun violence, racism, abuse, depression, opioids, pandemics—you name it. Life is hard. How do we cope? How do we get through it all? How do we heal the pain of our loneliness? How do we find, form, and keep family?

I still remember the first thing I uttered when told of my mother's passing. For hours after the accident, I feared the worst. I kept asking nurses at the hospital for details of my mother, but they kept putting me off. Finally, I fell asleep in a hospital room with fluorescent lighting beside my brother. Hours later, they woke me up, for my grandparents and uncle had arrived from Tennessee. Alongside them, a chaplain broke the news I'd expected. I'm not proud of my immediate reaction. I'm only being honest. A survival instinct kicked in. These words came out of me: "Who will be my mother?"

I couldn't comprehend surviving life without a mother, yet she was gone. What was I to do? I quickly realized the fragility of the family system. What happens when we place our foundational trust in our immediate family, only to lose them? Deep down, I understood I needed a family that could survive and outlast the brokenness of this world. I needed stability that included and yet exceeded my immediate family. For several years, I feared that something might happen to my father. I assume other kids in similar situations would have felt the same thing. I'd stand outside my elementary school waiting to be picked up in the afternoon. If my dad was just a couple of minutes late (which rarely happened), I began to panic. My brother would always tell me not to worry. He said Dad would come, and he did.

Still, in desperate conviction, I understood I needed a broader, larger family. Who would be my mother? My grandmother nurtured me with consistent love and steadfast devotion. A few years later, my dad remarried, and my second mom has enriched my life in innumerable ways. Yet in my life, the answer to this question has been filled by a group larger than any one person. Over time, I realized this truth. The church had become my mother.

I grew up at a very normal church of about three hundred or four hundred people. If you'd driven past it, nothing would have stood out to you. We met in a brick building. We had one of those old signs where you could put up the sermon title or a cliché message such as "CH _ _ CH

What's missing?" If you'd visited a service, very little would have stood out. We sang hymns and took Communion. A kind, generous preacher told *Reader's Digest*–type tales and encouraged us with Bible stories and verses. From an outside perspective, it probably would have all looked ordinary. Yet for me, it was family.

When I walked into my church building, I walked into a room full of uncles and aunts. In fact, I called many of them by those names, despite no blood relation. Everyone knew my name, and I knew their names. People smiled when they saw me. I loved being there. My buddies and I played lots of games around the church building. Once the adults were out in the vestibule talking after worship, we'd throw bouncy balls from the back of the auditorium and aim for the baptistry. If you ricocheted it in there, you got a point. If you got a clear splash with no bank, you got five points. An older member, Mr. Gifford, would confiscate our ball and scold us. Yet, we knew he cared about us. My childhood consisted of church potlucks, church cookouts, and church camp. I learned to hit the potluck line early before the Kentucky Fried Chicken ran out. I messed around with my friends and drank entirely too much Kool-Aid. On summer nights at church camp, we'd sing under the stars. It all felt so perfect, so edenic. I remember a song called, "Holy Father Grant Us Peace." We'd sing it right before bed. I don't know how we sounded, but to my childish ears, it sounded like angels. Surprising to me, God was granting me peace. I missed my mom, and yet I had my people. I felt welcome. If you wonder what it's like to grow up with hundreds of people that think you're awesome and hug you weekly, I can tell you. It's incredible. In fact, to this day, I feel most welcome and comfortable with the church.

To my surprise and dismay, as I entered college, I realized not everyone had that relational support growing up. I faced the truth that not everyone had healthy and positive church experiences. This devastated me. In fact, I count this realization as one of the greatest disappointments of my adult life. I don't know where I'd be without the support of the church. When I think that others not only didn't receive support but received harm, I'm sad beyond measure. Growing up, I'd been aware of my church's imperfections, even sins. Still, the good always seemed to outweigh the bad. Tragically, I realized that for many the bad had outweighed the good.

Believe me, I know the evils committed by the church, and I will not neglect them in these pages. Confession and repentance have taken place and must continue. Still, in my life, the church has always been there to meet me in my pain and loneliness. In the following pages, I will share the true stories of what this has looked like in my life. Many say that they were raised *in* the church. I say more than that. I was raised *by* the church. If I didn't have the church in my life, my life would have an enormous void.

In these pages, I want to make a bold claim. The church is the greatest social movement the world has ever known. The church offers a broad, comprehensive social web in a way unlike any other social grouping. To some, it will seem cliché or naïve. To others, it will seem utopian or idealistic. Still, spiritual community distinguishes itself from all other forms of social community. No other social group can give us community like a spiritual community—not our families, not our government/nation, and not our activism or hobby collectives. In normal, ordinary churches in your neighborhood, you can find spiritual family. You can find your people who will have your back.

Making this claim involves moving against the tide. While Jesus remains popular, the church's reputation has declined. In my life, I've witnessed the good, bad, and the ugly of local churches. In these pages, I'll explore why church can be so hard and complicated, while also making the case for the church as an agent of good. I'll explore the support and opportunities that normal churches provide, which no other social group provides in a similar way. Despite her failures, I'm still drawn to her. She's not perfect, but she's my mother.

2

Broken Humanity

In 1989, Don Henley released the classic song "End of the Innocence," featuring Bruce Hornsby on piano. That song always brings an instant dose of nostalgia for me, no matter when I hear it. About that time, around age eleven, I had my own loss-of-innocence experience. Most every day, I read the local newspaper. Whereas I mainly focused on the sports section, on this particular day, the front page caught my eye. A woman had been murdered in a local park. She had gone there to pray and read her Bible on a beautiful, sunny day. A man, deeply in debt, attempted to kidnap her and hold her for ransom. When the kidnapping didn't go as planned, he killed her. This rattled me, yet I was not prepared for what I read next. The article went on to report that the perpetrator served as a deacon at a local church. I recognized the name of the church. I knew people who went to that church, and he was their deacon. I thought of the deacons at my church. Did they kidnap women? Were they capable of murder? I grieved for the victim. I grieved for the perpetrator. I grieved for their families. I could not process the depths of this evil. I walked around for days in a daze. Although I knew none of them personally, this forever changed me.

You see, by age eleven, I already knew that bad things happened. After all, I'd experienced the death of my mother. My aunt fought cancer, which ultimately took her life. This was different, though. It wasn't that bad things happened. It was worse. Good people did bad things. A church deacon killed someone. This wasn't an outside job. Evil infiltrated the inside. Wickedness came from the very people who were supposed to fight it.

Growing up, I felt safe with my church. While it was not perfect, I felt comfortable. A sense of close camaraderie hovered around the community. I heard about bad things on the news. I read about evil things in the paper. I studied about wicked things in history books. But safe among my church, goodness reigned. Evil felt distant for me, but tragically not for everyone. For countless children, women, and men, the church has been anything but safe.

In the late summer of 2018, I travelled to Pittsburgh for the first time. I'd looked forward to the trip for nearly a year. Each summer, I go on a baseball trip with a group of guys, as we gradually attempt to visit all the Major League Baseball stadiums. I anticipated a relaxed weekend of Cracker Jacks, peanuts, stories, and nerdy baseball statistics. However, as we entered Pittsburgh, a dark cloud hovered. Earlier in the week, grand jury testimony came out detailing past patterns of abuse in the Catholic Church in and around the city.

Despite the abundance of abuse stories over the last twenty years, my heart still breaks every time. I grieve for the victims. I grieve for their families. I grieve for the calloused wickedness. I grieve for what this does to the reputation of Jesus and his community, the global church. To be clear, histories of abuse and harassment do not just exist in Catholic churches. After all, in previous weeks, my heart had broken at the revelations coming out of major Protestant churches. Moreover, the average person does not simply harbor suspicion at the offending churches. Many harbor suspicions at all churches. We're all in this together, and I confess I understand that reaction.

I lived in New England when the *Boston Globe* began to break the priest abuse scandal in 2002. I remember what it did to the credibility of the church—not just the Catholic Church, but all churches. At the time, I ministered at a congregation which had personally experienced leadership hypocrisy. In those times, I could sense the hemorrhaging of Christian credibility. One day, I had a conversation with Damon, a young man who attended our congregation with his mother and stepfather. As I got to know him better, the conversation turned to his father. He volunteered, "You know, my dad told me I should let him know if you ever try anything." Shocked at the insinuation that I might harbor that type of evil, I fumbled for a response. "Yeah, I understand. A lot of sad things have happened." As I thought about that later, I processed my emotions. My inner defensiveness abated. I admired the father for proactively preparing his son for a broken world. At the same, I remember feeling a deep disillusionment that the world had changed. Because of the sins of some, the cloud of suspicion hovers over all disciples of Jesus, over all churches.

On that late summer Sunday morning in Pittsburgh, as we walked to the game, I saw a Catholic church. I told my buddies I'd catch up with them later. I ducked into the church and realized I'd come in between masses. The sanctuary was empty. I walked up to a pew near the front. I got down on my knees, and I prayed. I begged God to forgive us. I apologized to Jesus for the way the American church has soiled his reputation. I asked God to purify and resurrect his body that we might again be the light of the world, salt of the earth, and a city on a hill. I beseeched the God of creation to fix our broken community of faith.

As the abuse and #ChurchToo scandals see no signs of abating, we have no other choice but contrite transparency. We can't be defensive. We may be frustrated that the actions of a few shape opinions on all of us, but the world doesn't need our frustration. It needs our confession and re-pentance. It's truly a time to lament. When people offer me their reasons for leaving the church, the brokenness of the church looms large. Through some painful trial and error, I've learned how unhelpful it is to react in a defensive manner. It's no help to immediately respond with "That wasn't me" or "The church has done a lot of good in the world." Our reaction must not be self-protection. We can't be in denial.

There's great irony in Christians refusing to face the broken-ness of the church. After all, one of the core doctrines of the faith lies in the truth that all sin. In the words of Paul in Romans 3:23, "All have sinned and fallen short of the glory of God." We see this illustrated on almost every page of the Bible. Sadly though, when it comes to abuse scandals, some Christians have too often been the last people to believe the sin detailed by victims. The denial lies in either naïveté or hypocrisy. Putting aside hypocrisy for now, biblical teaching should protect us from this naïveté. God is completely good. Humans are not. God makes us better, but we're never perfect.

The words of the Russian dissident Alexander Solzhenitsyn speak to this. "If only it were all so simple! If only there were evil people somewhere insidiously committing evil deeds, and it were necessary only to separate them from the rest of us and destroy them. But the line dividing good and evil cuts through the heart of every human being. And who is willing to destroy a piece of his own heart?"[1] We must model an honest authenticity.

---

1. Solzhenitsyn, *Gulag Archipelago*, 168.

We're sinners. Certainly, we should expect more from Christians, yet we should not be surprised when humans sin. It's what humans do.

The embrace of confession and repentance should lead to a posture of patient humility. No matter the situation or context, we must model humility. Too often, Christians hyper-focus on being right on an issue, while not considering posture. However, a posture of grace must be a nonnegotiable aspect of the faith.

I remember sitting down at Dunkin Donuts years ago with Ron, a twenty-something a few years removed from my youth ministry. I'd heard he no longer practiced his faith with a local church. In statistical terms, he'd become a "churchless Christian." I wanted to listen and hear how things were going. Eventually, he began to talk about his departure from church, which came on the heels of his parents' divorce. I'll never forget the simplicity of what he said. "When my mother left my dad, the church was rude to my mom. So, I quit going to church." On one hand, we might be tempted to give the church the benefit of the doubt. Perhaps some wanted to encourage her to stay in the marriage. Maybe some felt allegiance to the father. To be sure, I wasn't there, and it could have been all well intentioned. Perhaps there's a reasonable explanation for the church's behavior. Or maybe that's just an excuse. Because from his perspective, it's really simple. They said they loved everyone, and then they acted like jerks to his mom. Case closed. Church involvement over.

This is what happens when Christians overly fixate on being "right" but neglect the "right" posture. Likely, we can all share stories of a church being hyper-judgmental towards someone. Churches can focus so much on being biblical, advocating a correct position, that they don't act in biblical ways—gentle, patient, and holy. I confess that I maintain theological and ethical beliefs which most would regard as fairly traditional and consistent with church history. Still, I've been convicted in recent years that my notion of a biblical view offers no spiritual fruit without a biblical posture. Traditionally, many churches have ignored their own sins while focusing on the sins of the world. Traditionally, many churches have brought a mean-spirited, sometimes even hateful, tone to their interactions with others. Reversing course demands a nontraditional posture of mercy and grace.

I can't help but think of Jesus and the woman entrapped in adultery. You may remember this story from John 8. The religious teachers brought a woman to Jesus who had been caught in adultery. Clearly a setup, they enacted a plot to manipulate this young woman to publicly embarrass Jesus.

Instead, Jesus embarrassed them. He called them out on their hypocrisy in verse 7: "Let any one of you who is without sin be the first to throw a stone at her." One by one, they leave. Eventually, he turns to the woman for this beautiful interaction in verse 11. "Then neither do I condemn you," Jesus declared. "Go now and leave your life of sin."

I always notice Jesus' knack for balancing what I struggle so hard to balance. He encourages her to leave her life of sin. He's no moral relativist. Yet, he's not a pompous jerk either. It's possible to embrace ethical ideals yet be loving and merciful to everyone. The brokenness of the story looms large. It's unfair, messy, and even abusive. Yet, we've been telling this story over the centuries because Jesus took something broken and made it beautiful.

Standing up for "right" in a jerkish way does not imitate Christ. In addition, we all have to consider this: we could be wrong. I've been wrong before, and I'll be wrong again. I've changed my mind on a few things in my life, and I'm certain others have as well. This awareness should add to the welling up of humility inside us, which should shape our tone as well. I'm not suggesting that anyone waffle in their convictions or fall into total subjectivism. I'm simply suggesting that we resist seeing ourselves as final arbiters of truth. Once again, I believe in truth, yet I also believe in Paul's words from 1 Corinthians 13:12: "For now we see only a reflection as in a mirror; then we shall see face to face. Now I know in part; then I shall know fully, even as I am fully known." Every time I interact with someone, I discern my words carefully, and then I try to add a dose of humility. I don't always succeed, yet I continually pursue this goal.

Too often, Christians have said one thing and done another. Hypocrisy looms large. I'm reminded of a friend's church years ago. A woman at the church taught a teen girls class on purity and saving oneself for marriage. Meanwhile, she carried on an affair the entire time. I've seen elders claim the moral high ground on worship style only for their affairs and pornography addictions to come out later. For a while, I ran this experiment. I counted the number of weeks that a high-profile religious leader got exposed for a public transgression such as financial impropriety, sexual indiscretion, or an offensive social media post. I quit counting at nine weeks. It got too depressing.

In the theology courses I teach at Lipscomb University, we often discuss the students' understanding of Jesus as well as their religious background. Every time, I'm amazed and devastated at the sheer weight and damage of hypocrisy. In my experience, Jesus and core, classic Christian teaching remain appealing. Sadly though, the chronic pain and stress caused by hypocrisy presents too much baggage. In some, it's almost like encountering someone with PTSD.

The other day, I sat in a local library working on my computer. Martha, a friend I hadn't seen in a while, walked in. A couple of years ago, I knew she had been looking for a new church home. A minute or so into the conversation, I asked if she'd landed at any particular church or had gone back to her former congregation. Instantly, tears flowed. She had been mistreated and wronged by Christians. It severely impacted her ability to trust and rest in a congregation. She remains haunted by hypocrisy. Streams of emotion lay just below the surface. One simple question brought it all out. Every single day, she walks around with this pain.

The body of Christ is broken. There's no escaping it. The church must repent. Before we repent, nothing else really matters. So, let me take my turn. I am part of the church, and the church has sinned. I confess that the church has justified egregious wars. I confess the evils of the Crusades and Inquisition. I confess that the church has abused and then covered it up. I confess that the church has turned a blind eye too often to sexism. I confess that the church has been racist. I confess that the church has incurred numerous scarlet letters, ranging from shaming unwed mothers to homophobia. I confess that many times the church has said one thing and done another. I confess that the church has judged the world's sins but ignored her own. I confess that when I see the bumper sticker "Lord save us from your followers," I get it. I confess that the church is broken.

Let me be clear. I don't apologize for Jesus. I don't apologize for the Sermon on the Mount or any part of his teaching. I don't apologize for the cross. I don't apologize for the Bible, even the hard parts or the parts I don't like. But I am sorry for the harm Christians have caused.

The world is broken. Both human experience and the Bible tell us this. Jesus called the church to continue his work in mending this broken world. Yet, instead of being a part of the solution, we've too often been part of the problem. Friends, if you're angry, you are right to be angry. I pray you will hear my confession, for nothing that follows matters without it.

This morning, I walked to the end of my driveway, reached down, and grabbed the morning paper. Yes, I know, I'm old school. I like the feel of the paper mixed with the smell of my morning coffee. In this morning's paper, a high-profile Christian got exposed for leading a double life. The truth came out. His hypocritical lies unraveled. As I sat there reading, I was not surprised. Then, out of nowhere, a familiar tune popped in my head. A painful nostalgia crept in. The church is not innocent, and neither am I.

3

Lost Community

BALLOONS MAKE ME SMILE. There's just something about a balloon that lightens the mood. They offer a sign of joy, even frivolity, in the midst of all that ails us. Even now, I keep packs of balloons around the house. When my girls ask for balloons, I want to be ready. One memory of balloons rises above all others.

The day after my mother died, I went to the hospital to visit my father. Banged up from the accident, his injuries ultimately kept him there for a week. My grandparents took me and my brother to visit him. As we got off the elevator on his floor, a crying woman walked up to me and my brother. She held balloons. I didn't know who she was, but through her tears, she gave each of us a colorful balloon. I should point out that these were not cheap balloons. They were the really nice expensive ones that parents don't often spring for at birthday parties. I can't remember if I thanked her or not. It was all so awkward and weird. Quickly, she moved on. Then, it dawned on me. I'd seen her face before.

I'd seen her the day prior. This same face looked in our car window. After the accident, several cars stopped to check on us. I remember her face. I remember how she looked, an expression of panic amidst a desire to put on a brave face. She lovingly helped us get out of the shattered car. My brother even remembers me siting in her lap as she tried to distract us from the horrific scene. As an adult, she knew what I wouldn't be told for hours. Apparently, she tracked us down to the hospital. She wanted to find us. She wanted to give us balloons, the nice expensive kinds that I rarely if ever received. I liked that balloon.

Later that day, we drove the several-hour drive back home. We stayed with friends from church for a few days. Then, my grandparents stayed at our house with us. We made it through the funeral, and finally my dad got released from the hospital and came home. Through all of it, I had my balloon. As I remember, it stayed inflated for quite a while. Eventually, it sunk to the floor, but I still kept it. I had that balloon for a long time. I like balloons because they remind me of that kind nameless woman. When I felt alone, she gave me a balloon. Because of her kindness, I felt less alone. I'll never forget her. Why do we do things like that? Why did she pull over? Why did she run over and look into our car? Why did she put all the effort into tracking us down at the hospital? Why did she buy us balloons?

Humans are social animals. We are hardwired for community. God designed us to be in relationship. Going deeper, God exists as relationship. Therefore, if humans have been created in the image of God, humans exist as relational beings. Christians trace the human condition back to the nature of God. The Bible teaches us that God is one. In Deuteronomy 6:4, we read, "Hear oh Israel, the Lord our God, the Lord is one." God is a singular, unified being. At the same time, the Bible teaches us that God exists as Father, Son, and Holy Spirit. In Matthew 28:19, we find, "Therefore go and make disciples of all nations, baptizing them in the name of the Father and of the Son and of the Holy Spirit." We normally think of this as the Trinity. God is both one and many. It's a paradox for sure, and yet Christians explore it for great meaning and understanding.

Humans are image-bearers of this God. Therefore, deep in our being, we simultaneously exist as both individual and communal beings. We need alone time and social time. Both are embedded in our nature, our condition. Without community, we will struggle to be healthy. Without adequate boundaries and individual awareness, including alone time, we will struggle to thrive. We need both because God is both.

Every Wednesday, my local church gathers for a brown bag dinner before our midweek prayer and study time. People steadily flow into our church facility with their food and decompress from busy days at work. It's one of my favorite times of the week. Kids run all over the place. Teens huddle in the corner to tell stories from school. The adults tell jokes, talk current events, and share tales from work. I look forward to it all week. Normally, my friend Ryan comes to this. After he finishes his meal, though, he disappears. He goes upstairs and sits in our sanctuary, often without turning on the lights. He sits there and enjoys the quiet. I'm embarrassed to say that many times I've gone to find him and engage him in conversation. I didn't want him to be alone. Slowly, I got it, though. He needs that solo time, and so do I. Even as I emphasize community, I don't want to neglect the need for a healthy rhythm. We need both.

As I often am, I'm drawn to the words of Dietrich Bonhoeffer, about whom I'll say more later. In his *Life Together*, he says this about community.

> Let him who cannot be alone beware of community . . . Let him who is not in community beware of being alone . . . Each by itself has profound perils and pitfalls. One who wants fellowship without solitude plunges into the void of words and feelings, and the one who seeks solitude without fellowship perishes in the abyss of vanity, self-infatuation and despair.[1]

Notice the "each by itself." We need to remember our individuality. We cannot lose sight of the self. Yet, we're our most healthy self when we connect with each other. In fact, we were created to be together in community.

No one lived into this balance better than Jesus. He spent his life making community. He intentionally ate with tax collectors, prostitutes, and even hostile religious leaders. He called disciples to follow him. Yet, he often wandered off from those same disciples to spend time in prayer. He modeled the balance that we need. Of course, this will look different in each person. We have to consider the uniqueness of personality. Still, we must lean into rhythm and balance.

American culture is out of balance. The rugged individual mystique remains one of the hallmarks of American culture. We continue to watch Westerns with cowboys dependent on no one. We watch survivalist reality TV shows. Often, we think of not needing anyone as a life goal. We dream of getting to a point where we can completely take care of ourselves financially, physically, and emotionally. When sociologists and psychologists scale countries on individualism/collectivism, the United States always shows up as the most individualistic culture. We believe we can take care of ourselves, but we can't. We need community, and we must expose the myth of total self-reliance.

In my high school English class, I read Henry David Thoreau's *Walden, or Life in the Woods*. In the work, Thoreau details the two-plus years he spent alone in a cabin out in the woods. As a teen, I read that and dreamed of striking out on my own. Thoreau's words of introspection and exploration fed my zeal for the individualist/self-reliant ethos. About five

1. Bonhoeffer, *Life Together*, 77–78.

years after high school, in 2001, while visiting a friend in Massachusetts, we went in search of Walden Pond. Of course, a remote area in Thoreau's time now lies in the Boston suburbs. Still, much of it has been preserved. As we walked out to the location of his cabin and took in the tour, the veil lifted from the illusion. I discovered a breakdown in the mystique that I didn't remember from before. Thoreau spent those two years in a cabin two miles from his parents. On occasion, he went home for dinner. What? The guy who helped motivate me to move hundreds and hundreds of miles from my family only went as far as a half-hour stroll. My vision of Thoreau not needing anyone was replaced by a guy who kept walking home for his mother's cooking. Yes, Thoreau had a legitimate experience of reflection in the woods. At the same time, Thoreau needed people. That's not a bad thing. In fact, it's a true thing. We all need people.

Unfortunately, since the 1960s, American culture has gradually experienced a systemic loss in community. In his seminal work *Bowling Alone*, sociologist Robert Putnam observed that commitment to social structures has declined over the last couple of generations.[2] From civic clubs to churches to sports leagues to political parties, adults are far less committed to involvement and volunteerism. As Putnam alludes to in his book title, Americans still bowl, but they more often bowl alone. I like to read the Sunday newspaper, and I always look at the obituaries. For those ages seventy and older, I'm amazed at how many club and organizational memberships they list in the obituary. Almost all list a local church, as well as things ranging from the Lion's Club to the Rose Garden Association. My generation doesn't join organizations at the same rate.

Rampant distrust of institutions fueled this decline of community. The bigger an institution became, the more loathing it fostered. This has only increased in my lifetime. On a daily basis, I hear a consistent frustration and cynicism over essential institutions. We complain about healthcare, education, government, and religion. Notice how people employ the adjective "big" to foster negativity, such as "big business" or "big government." Overall, Americans express dissatisfaction at once trusted institutions and desire a different future. To be clear, legitimate reasons led to this. Many of our most trusted organizations have let us down. Various reforms and changes have been needed. Yet, as we've retreated from institutions and organizations, we must honestly look at what we've turned to instead.

---

2. Putnam, *Bowling Alone*, 25.

For one, we've placed more expectations on our marriages. We now look to our spouse to be our soulmate, life partner, best friend, lover, co-parent, and spiritual confidant, while eagerly sharing in all of our hobbies. It's no wonder marital satisfaction proves elusive for many with those lofty expectations. Likewise, we've heightened our expectations of work. Beyond supporting our families and communities, we now look for purpose every day in our jobs. While I affirm the desire for meaningful work, the hyper-focus on purpose in career often reaches unrealistic heights. Our families and jobs were not designed to meet all of our social needs.

I believe God designed church to meet many of these social needs, and yet it has suffered the same institutional suspicion and withdrawal as other organizations. Since I serve as a minister, religion and faith practice frequently come up in conversations. Often, people express frustration and dissatisfaction about their church experience. I've grown accustomed to people confiding in me that they no longer identify with or attend a specific congregation. Besides the sin and hypocrisy of the church, other reasons show up for the withdrawal. Many leave over a perceived anti-science bent or at least a sense of having to choose between science and faith. Others reference the church's inability or unwillingness to walk with them through life's pain and provide a sensible framework for interpreting suffering. Some have left over the increasing politicization of churches and church leaders. They may resent hearing politics from the pulpit, or they may resent the unwillingness of the church to speak out about certain issues. Some would cite unwillingness to adjust to prevailing gender or sexual cultural norms, and some might cite conforming to those gender and sexual norms as a reason for leaving. People quit participation in local churches for a variety of reasons.

American culture has pursued a widespread deconstruction of social institutions including the church. I began to notice this in the years after the abuse scandals of the early 2000s and the rising role of faith in political conversations and elections. Among Christians, it became more and more acceptable to call out the church. I'm thankful for that. We should call out the church, but over time I became concerned. Instead of a precision strategy of calling out the church for specific sins, many affirmed a blanket strategy of default suspicion towards church. As the spirit of deconstruction grew steam, I realized many had no plans to rebuild. To them, the church was too far gone. This was not about reform or renewal, but demolition. To save the Jesus movement, Christians would have to separate Jesus from the church.

As deconstructionists promoted this effort, they pointed to an influential advocate: Jesus himself. After all, throughout the Gospels, Jesus harshly rebuked the Jewish religious leaders. Specifically, he called out their hypocrisy and mistreatment of the marginalized. Here's a short sampling from Matthew 23:13-15:

> "Woe to you, teachers of the law and Pharisees, you hypocrites! You shut the door of the kingdom of heaven in people's faces. You yourselves do not enter, nor will you let those enter who are trying to. Woe to you, teachers of the law and Pharisees, you hypocrites! You travel over land and sea to win a single convert, and when you have succeeded, you make them twice as much a child of hell as you are."

It's not exactly the Jesus we often picture, yet it's real. Jesus pulled no punches with these leaders. They mistreated people, and Jesus refused to be silent about the brokenness. Many seek to channel this side of Jesus. In their minds, the most Christlike posture centers on a default antagonism towards religious groups.

At the same time, deconstructionists gravitate towards Jesus' words of encouragement to a group outside the religious institutions of his day: the marginalized. Jesus frequently ate with the sinners and appeared far more comfortable with those outside the religious establishment. Consider Jesus' words in Matthew 21:31-32.

> Jesus said to them, "Truly I tell you, the tax collectors and the prostitutes are entering the kingdom of God ahead of you. For John came to you to show you the way of righteousness, and you did not believe him, but the tax collectors and the prostitutes did. And even after you saw this, you did not repent and believe him."

Jesus not only affirms these marginalized disciples but gives them a preferential posture. In our day, many have interpreted this in the following way. We should harbor default suspicion towards churches and offer a preferential posture for those who have left church. In various ways, I've heard this—ranging from direct messaging to indirect insinuation—at churches and Christian conferences for about fifteen years now. It has predictable results. A steady diet of this leads one to leave the church and join those who aren't criticized. After all, who wouldn't want to join the group Jesus actually likes?

Let me be clear. I believe we should call out the sin of religions institutions as Jesus did. I believe we should welcome those who seek the kingdom but have been marginalized. We must follow Jesus' lead on this, and yet we must consider a third group. Jesus spent a lot of time with a group other than the religious leaders and marginalized: the apostles. They would be the leaders of his movement after his death, and we should notice his posture towards them.

So how does Jesus talk to the apostles? We see considerable nuance. We see a blend of both blistering critique and compassionate care. Consider Jesus' interaction with Peter in Matthew 16. When Peter confesses his faith that Jesus is the Messiah, he receives affirmation. However, when he questions Jesus' talk of the cross, Jesus refers to him as Satan. Why the mixed tone? Jesus had the long game of reform in mind. He both deconstructed and reconstructed. He both critiqued and encouraged. Jesus believed in and practiced spiritual community. So, when we call out sin and hypocrisy, we imitate Jesus. But also, to imitate Jesus, we must seek to build up the community. While Christians can kindly debate the nature of the church's organization, it's clear that Jesus trained his followers to continue his movement.

My discomfort with deconstruction absent reconstruction found clarity in a February 2012 *New York Times* column by David Brooks.[3] He responded to a January YouTube video by Jefferson Bethke entitled "Why I Hate Religion, but Love Jesus."[4] As of this writing, the video has over thirty-four million views. To be clear, I sympathize with many of Bethke's critiques, yet I am uncomfortable with the end result. I could not blame someone if they walked away with the message that we should simply follow Jesus individually and stay away from church. In his column, Brooks seeks to engage the climate where people "are disgusted by current institutions, but then they are vague about what sorts of institutions should replace them." He later adds, "Effective rebellion isn't just expressing your personal feelings. It means replacing one set of authorities and institutions with a better set of authorities and institutions." We need community. Admittedly, we have all experienced the failings of community, and certainly no authority or institution will ever be perfect. Yet, if we care about Jesus, we must continue his movement. Cynicism and sarcasm will not get us out of this mess. The answer to the problem lies in rebuilding healthy communities, not doubling down on individualism and isolation.

3. Brooks, "How to Fight the Man."
4. Bethke, "Why I Hate Religion."

You were created in the image of God. Christians believe God is both one and three. God is singular and plural. You are an individual meant for community. You need a healthy balance of both. Look at your life. Listen to your body. Consider the tough choices you might need to make to get balance. You will not achieve health until you have both. You are like God, and this is what God is like. God lives in community. If you don't live in community, a part of you is missing.

On that August morning in Pittsburgh from last chapter, I walked out of the church somber. I wondered if I'd see the restoration of the church's credibility in my lifetime. Will I see the reconstruction of the Christian community in America? Within a half hour, I caught up with my buddies. We joined the streams of thousands headed for the baseball game. Surrounded by baseball fans, I felt a deep camaraderie. I partook in the joys of the community. I walked around visiting holy relics, the statues of great Pittsburgh Pirates. I ate of the traditional sacrament of ballpark food. I sang "Take Me Out to the Ballgame" at the top of my lungs. When the home team won, I cheered. I felt part of the community, and it felt good. This community did not come to exist overnight. As I spoke with locals, many had been Pirates fans for years. Moreover, even as my friends and I were not Pirates fans, we'd been immersed in baseball culture and ritual for years. This experience of community flowed out of deep history and commitment.

We're experiencing a pervasive loss of community in our culture because we've been hurt by previous forms of community. Our pain has caused us to lash out, which is understandable. However, our pain has forced us inward into isolation and individualism. Our pain has made us suspicious of making the long-term sacrifices that bring about community. Our imperfect churches have hurt many people. I humbly suggest that the appropriate response is a time of mourning, repentance, and then steadfast renewal and reform. Endless critique will not get us there. We must balance the prophetic rebuke with the embrace of the shepherd. We can't complain our way out of this. We must rebuild.

Driving home that day, I reflected on community. We long for it, even as it slips through our fingers. We crave it, but we don't want to work too hard for it. We want to consume it. None of us got into that Pirates game for free. None of us ate free hot dogs as we watched millionaire athletes. We felt real community, but we had to pay for it. We bought it. In America, we like our sense of community packaged and sold in tidy, curated ways. What happens when Americans respond to the breakdown in community through the impulse of consumerism? We'll look at that in the next chapter.

4

Consumerism

FOR THE FIRST TWENTY-TWO years of my life, I lived in Tennessee and Texas. Most everyone I knew went to church. People talked fairly openly about faith. Most towns boasted the proverbial church on every corner. Whether you went often or not, when asked, most everyone claimed a local congregation of some sort. However, it seemed rare for folks to attend the same congregation for their entire adult life. Church hopping was fairly common for a variety of reasons, some theological and some trivial. I had friends who changed churches for doctrinal reasons. I had a friend who changed churches because he wanted a church with a basketball gym. Specifically, in Nashville, church culture appeared fairly competitive.

When I moved to New England, I immediately sensed a difference. While Christian identification continues at a higher rate than some parts of the world, it's not the American South. At first glance, it seemed like the Dunkin Donuts franchises outnumbered the churches. Because of this, the same level of church competition did not exist. Since options proved fewer, I found people to be far less picky. I remember few if any threats, ultimatums, or emergency meetings to keep a disgruntled family. People appeared to have fewer expectations and therefore higher levels of satisfaction. I'll come back to this connection between expectations and degrees of satisfaction.

I noticed another thing. Because the options for leaving were fewer, people were forced to stay and work out their differences. This created a "big tent" vibe. While the congregation certainly had its style and personality, we maintained a greater breadth of theological diversity than other congregations I had experienced. Once, I remember asking an elder an opinion about the latest controversy, mainly among big Southern churches. He looked at me with a puzzled expression. "We don't have time for that up here."

After six years, Beth and I moved back to Nashville, where we'd grown up. We moved for her teaching job with the plan that I'd find a ministry job in due time. For the first time in our married life, we were not tied to one congregation. We could visit around and enjoy the spiritual feast of the "buckle" of the Bible Belt.

Our first Sunday, we picked a large, successful church we'd heard a lot about and set out. Fairly quickly, our car came to a standstill. Dumbfounded, I couldn't figure out the reason for the traffic. Who ever heard of a traffic jam on a Sunday morning? However, on a main route in the city lies multiple, enormous church buildings. Most had officers directing traffic with cones planted all over the road. I had no box to put this in. A reverse culture shock set in. For weeks, we partook of excellent worship and powerful preaching, but we couldn't figure out how to meet people. It felt impressive but hollow. It was big and flashy, not simple. People were nice and friendly, but with little guidance on how to connect, make friends, and participate in ministry. Honestly, it all felt vacuous. We felt incredibly lonely.

During this time, Christian friends and family would ask us if we'd chosen a church. In response, I found myself mimicking language I'd often heard in Southern church culture. "We're still shopping around." The language of church shopping reveals a lot. Consumerist language brings more baggage than we realize. When we apply the lens of consumerism to our search for community, a strange thing happens. We've immediately lowered our chance of finding it. An inverse relationship exists between consumerism and communal satisfaction. By definition, consumerism creates dissatisfaction amidst a veiled promise of satisfaction. It cultivates pickiness, even selfishness, in ways that makes contentment challenging and difficult.

For example, I've noticed a common thread when people tell me about their church experiences. Most of these personal accounts come from neighborhoods with abundant and diverse churches. However, I have found that few people seem satisfied with their faith community. When the conversation comes up, a flood of discontentment streams out. Many tell me they can't find a church. Often, the language of needs comes up. "We need this." "It doesn't meet our needs," etc. Why do Christians surrounded by churches struggle to find deep spiritual community? Think long and hard about this. Deep cultural trends have brought us to this point.

In the early 1970s, savvy students of culture saw the wave of church disengagement on the horizon. To their credit, they sought to stem the tide through creativity and ingenuity while continuing historic practices. Likely, the two most well-known examples include Bill Hybels, who started Willow Creek Community Church outside Chicago, and Rick Warren, who started Saddleback Community Church in Orange County. With the upmost intentionality, they began to cultivate churches that attracted those who had given up on church. Instead of trying to convince people to come to church as it was, they sought to create a church that the "churchless Christians" and "Nones" of their day desired. By and large, this proved successful, not only for "churchless Christians" and "Nones," but for those attending traditional churches. In many ways, these church plants served as the "research and development" wing of the church. Today, many congregations embrace styles and trends cultivated in this time period—from worship style to small groups to nonconfrontational language.

This coincided with the church growth movement, as well as the homogenous unit principle (the idea that targeted, specific demographics grow quicker than sporadic, diverse demographics). They leveraged business strategies, cultivated church brands, and catered to predetermined demographic groups. For example, let's plant a suburban church which caters to the taste of Baby Boomers. Let's plant a Generation X church in a slowly gentrifying neighborhood with music styles to match. Phrases such as "seeker sensitive" and "meeting their needs" became all the rage. Elements of these churches include worshipping in spaces other than a traditional church building, moving from organs to praise bands, casual dress, and less religious jargon in the preaching. These congregations engaged popular culture. More than that, they intentionally sought to connect with youth culture. Much of the ethos of these churches came from the youth ministry models of the 1960s and 1970s.

Overall, these trendsetters streamlined the process of church participation. In some ways, it was church made simple, fun, and easy. To be clear, many came to Christ through this. To be honest, much good happened through these efforts. I'm thankful for their hearts and service. I confess that ignoring culture and doubling down on the status quo of church brings poor fruit of its own. But looking back now, as we do in any trend, we see weaknesses. We notice pitfalls that would have been difficult to recognize at the time.

The paradigm of consumerism often brings short-term gratification alongside long-term dissatisfaction. Put differently, by in essence affirming and cultivating the consumerist side of American Christians, we have opened Pandora's box. Many modern-day churchgoers simply can't be satisfied anymore. Awhile back, I chatted with a friend who had planted a new church. For many healthy reasons, this congregation experienced rapid growth and manifested considerable good influence in the neighborhood and world. I'm thankful for this church and other church plants like it. As we discussed his ministry one day, he shared the philosophy behind his church. "We planted a church for people who won't go to any other church." On one hand, I totally understood. They planted a church for "churchless Christians" or those on the edge of being done with church. But on the other hand, I wondered about something lurking beneath the surface.

I have a sense many people hear it this way: "We understand why you won't go to any other church. We don't want to either. This church will be different." It's an exciting and bold promise. What if I can have spiritual community in the way I desire it without the brokenness and sin of my past spiritual communities? It sounds awesome. Where can I sign up? But there's a problem, a very human problem. Ultimately, imperfect people cannot make perfect communities. What happens when this new church inevitably falls short?

Too often, our expectations for what we want in a church can make finding one almost impossible. Let me share the types of things I often hear.

- "I want a nonjudgmental church."
- "I want a church that stands up for justice."
- "I want a church with a strong children's ministry or teen ministry."
- "I want a church close to where I live."
- "I want good preaching."
- "I want contemporary praise music" or some particular style.
- "I want a church with diversity."
- "I want a church in my denomination to make my parents happy but progressive enough to suit my spouse."
- "I want a church with lots of resources and programs for my family."

- "I want a church that doesn't constantly ask for money."
- "I want a church with politics that match my own."
- "I want a church where I can make deep relationships."
- "I want a church that doesn't put pressure on my involvement."

These desires seem understandable to me. However, if the list gets too long and elaborate, the possibility of thriving in a church begins to diminish.

I'm not immune from this. My expectations for church have loomed large in my interactions with her over the years. Gradually, I saw my expectations sucking the life from my joy in the community. I wanted my community to stay true to certain nonnegotiable Christian truths while adjusting on some cultural traditions. Of course, I wanted to personally decide on the difference in the two. Doesn't everybody? I wanted a close community that I could call at any moment, but I didn't want a community that called me too often and intruded on my personal life. I wanted more than they could give, more than anyone could give.

At some point in this journey, a friend had me read Dietrich Bonhoeffer's *Life Together*. Bonhoeffer, a German pastor and theologian, famously refused to embrace the Nazis in the 1930s and 1940s. As part of the Confessing Church, the minority of German churches openly opposed to Hitler, he led an underground seminary to train church leaders. These German Christians made the Sermon on the Mount ground zero for faith and practice as they sought to be salt and light in the darkest of times. In those days, Bonhoeffer meditated often on the dynamics of community. In those intense times, they certainly brought heightened expectations of community to their interactions. Bonhoeffer encouraged them to consider the power of those expectations. I remember the first time I read these words some fifteen years ago. "Those who love their dream of a Christian community more than they love the Christian community itself become destroyers of that Christian community even though their personal intentions may be ever so honest, earnest and sacrificial."[1]

The only solution, according to Bonhoeffer, lay in the ability to love the community for what it was, not just for what you wanted it to be. As I read these words years ago, scales fell from my eyes. Sadly, too often, I'd approached the local church with expectations. I would form it into the community of my dreams. The results were exactly as Bonhoeffer predicted.

1. Bonhoeffer, *Life Together*, 27.

I grew frustrated. The church grew frustrated. The community that we did share became compromised by mutual frustration. Years later, in my current ministry, I find myself telling others. "Let's love this congregation for what it is, not what it could be. Let's commit to it in its current state, not our desired state." On occasion, I do counsel people to leave a church. At times, a change proves necessary. You should not stay long-term in an unhealthy situation. Still, we must discern carefully to avoid the pitfalls of consumerism.

Treating Christians like customers may provide temporary gains, but it proves devasting in the end. Many of my friends work in college and university life. Over the last couple of decades, higher education has faced skyrocketing costs and increased competition for students. One posture change has been an increased treatment of the student as customer. You can see this in the development of entertainment programs ancillary to education such as rock-climbing walls, goat yoga, and posh dorm rooms. A professor friend recounted this exchange. A student with poor study habits and a subpar academic performance asked for a reference. My friend admitted that he could give a reference, but it'd likely be average at best. Angrily, as if writing to the customer relations department, the student suggested that he'd paid good money to attend the school and deserved a good reference. The customer paradigm attracts with promises to fulfill combined with easy access. After a customer has entered into that community, they expect to receive the promise and respond negatively when it's not experienced.

Years ago, a professor in seminary recounted a conversation he'd had with a church planter. With an ample dose of sarcasm, he said, "Want to know how to start a megachurch? You just need three things: Music so good that people would pay for it, a charismatic, polished speaker, and clean women's restrooms." I must confess that I'm not opposed to any of that. I like a good clean restroom as much as the next person. At the same time, notice the consumerism at play. It centers on comfort and ease. It focuses on attraction, not participation. To be clear, this is not about size. Small churches can have a consumerist culture, just as large churches can have a participatory culture. Discernment is key.

You can see how the embrace of the consumerist model parallels the type of thing I heard when I waited tables during and right after college. "The customer is always right." I said that and embraced that as a waiter, even as I knew it wasn't true. Frequently, my customers were wrong. But, as they were consumers, I put up with it for the money I received. Is this a way to do church? You can't treat someone like a customer one day and expect them to be a disciple the next day. Church made easy does not prepare one for the difficult work of carrying the cross.

To understand this more, perhaps we should take a step back. The consumer paradigm of American life centers on the development of more and more choices. It's one of the main ways that Americans express creativity and uniqueness, through the cultivation and consummation of choice. Tied up in all of this lies the assumption that more choices will produce more happiness. Research actually shows the opposite. Our plethora of choices plays a role in our dissatisfaction and loneliness. Jacqueline Olds and Richard Schwartz explore this in their book, *The Lonely American*. "Problems come when the number of choices goes from a few to many. When people have lots of choices, they worry more about making the wrong choices. That worry trumps the joyful sense of freedom."[2] As an example, I'm old enough to remember when soda companies began packaging cherry and diet versions of their drink. The addition of a few choices added some excitement and satisfaction. Yet, when I go to the drink aisle of a grocery store these days, I feel a bit overwhelmed. It's too much. When I let my kids drink a soda on a special occasion, the breadth of choices almost paralyzes them. For many, it leads to pickiness and dissatisfaction. As Olds and Schwartz say later, "Common sense tells us that having more choices is better than having less. Science contradicts that. Yet most people stick to common sense."[3] The proliferation of church choice has given us a sugar rush, a short-term gain followed by a long-term trajectory of dissatisfaction.

Consumerism does not mesh well with discipleship. Years ago, while serving as a youth minister, a young man came up to me asking if the teens could start a Bible study in another part of the church building during the Sunday sermon. Since the entire church normally met together for worship, I hadn't anticipated this request. "Why?" I asked. "Is there something wrong with the sermon?" "Well," he said, "the preacher just started a six-week marriage series, and none of us are married. I thought we might study something that applies to us." Confused even more, I calmly responded, "I understand, but you may be married someday. Besides, not every sermon is going to be everyone's favorite." Frustrated, he pleaded, "I just don't think I'm going to get anything out of it." There it is, that familiar line we've all heard, "get something out of it." In any conversation, it signals you've entered a consumer dynamic.

2. Olds and Schwartz, *Lonely American*, 138.
3. Olds and Schwartz, *Lonely American*, 138.

I don't fault the young man. With endless age targeted programming with consumer packaging, we'd trained him to have that attitude.

Consumerism leverages expectations to create desire. However, once expectations have been incited, the failure to meet those expectations kills enjoyment. Too often, it can stunt growth, and I've even seen it create hostility. Once again, while short-term gain based on instant gratification may occur, religious consumerism often leaves one worse than when they started.

A few years ago, some college students encouraged me to check out the Netflix drama *Black Mirror*. Specifically, they recommended the episode "Be Right Back," which messed me up in all the right ways. In the episode, a woman mourns the sudden death of her husband. Sometime into her grief process, she discovers a company that can create an artificial intelligence that resembles deceased loved ones. She orders a "robot" replica of her husband based on his online social media history. At first, it's like resurrection. She jumps back into the relationship as if nothing has ever gone wrong. Eventually, his "artificial" nature surfaces. He's similar to her husband, yet not the same. Having already grown attached and unable to face the prospect of a second grief process, she decides to keep him at home. During the day, she goes to work and lives her life as a single person. At night, though, when she's lonely, she pulls him out for companionship. By the end, you see the ways the promise of technology has relationally stunted her grief process and compromised her joy. She's unable to move on towards a hopeful future.

I'm convinced we've done the same thing. Out of an understandable desire to get more people involved in church, we chased the sugar rush of religious consumerism. Church is not an experience to consume but a community in which we participate. Jesus did not come to make us religious consumers but sacrificial disciples. You can't buy your way into meaningful community. Our strategy failed. The result is this: We're incredible lonely, and we can't consume our way out of it.

5

Loneliness

I GRADUATED FROM COLLEGE in May of 2000. Like many college students, I had an active social life. My roommates felt like brothers. We took crazy weekend road trips, did harmless pranks, drank milkshakes, and played intramural sports and video games together. Daily, I hung out with people who supported and challenged me in indescribable ways. I had dozens of friends and had access to relational connections any time I desired. While I experienced inevitable ups and downs, those four years offered much joy and shaped me in lifelong ways.

But then, I left it all. After graduation, I drove almost a thousand miles back to my hometown, to the house I grew up in. That drive was painful. I felt physically sick as I looked in the rearview mirror. In my mind, I had little choice. My college friends scattered throughout the country taking jobs, and since I didn't have one yet I went back to wait tables at a restaurant just two miles from my childhood home.

I felt an intense sense of loneliness, and then it got worse. After a summer back home waiting tables, I took a job one thousand miles in the opposite direction from where I'd gone to school. That Labor Day weekend, I packed a U-Haul and began the drive alone. Sure, I felt a tinge of excitement and enthusiasm. At the same time, a deep awareness came over me. I had left all my social support to move to a place where I knew no one. Away from the social apparatus of a college campus, I had to socially start over in a more challenging environment.

Having no GPS device, I printed off online directions before I left home. I knew no one whom I could ask, "Is this the best way to get there?"

The route took me through the heart of New York City, over the George Washington Bridge. At a toll both, I faced an $18.75 charge, driving a U-Haul towing my vehicle. I lived on a shoestring budget, and this toll charge floored me. I can laugh now, but at the time it rattled me. To make matters worse, I drove through the city at rush hour. At one point, the car in front of me suddenly braked. Unable to stop in time, I swerved without checking into the left lane. Miraculously, I didn't hit anyone. Still, I felt so afraid. I'd entered unfamiliar territory, and I didn't know anyone. If I had a wreck or any trouble at all, I had no one to call.

I felt completely alone. Hours later, I pulled up to the little New England cottage I'd rented about a twenty-minute drive from my new job. I walked into an empty living room. I pulled the mattress out of the truck and set it down in an empty bedroom. Silence filled the room. Isolation overwhelmed me. I felt a deep physiological alarm going off inside of me.

Now certainly, many have experienced far worse. Many have traveled much greater distances to far more extreme circumstances. I don't say this because my experience proves unique, but because it's so common. At some point, we all experience loneliness. If our loneliness continues to deepen, we may face drastic consequences. If our loneliness becomes chronic, we may even face undesirable health consequences.

In January of 2018, I heard news that surprised me. Teresa May, the prime minister of the United Kingdom, announced a public health crisis in the United Kingdom. This growing crisis affected over nine million people and demanded immediate intervention. What was this public health crisis? Cancer? Violent extremism or indoctrination? Opioid abuse? Certainly all these deserve attention, but none gained her attention on this day. Instead, May wielded the power of her office to shine attention on a growing, surprising, and dangerous crisis in our world—loneliness. I'd never thought of loneliness as a health crisis, and I was unprepared for what I'd soon discover about the unhealthy ramifications.

What exactly are we talking about? To learn more about this, I recommend *Loneliness*, by John T. Cacioppo and William Patrick. Loneliness is one's perception and experience of a lack of relational interaction and support. A clear difference exists between loneliness and being alone. You probably know someone who lives alone, loves being alone, and yet rarely feels lonely. At the same time, you probably have a friend who works with people, lives with a spouse and kids, rarely spends time alone, and yet still feels incredibly lonely. It's the "lonely in a crowd" phenomenon. In fact, overall, on average, lonely and non-lonely people spend statistically the same amount of time around people.[1] When we speak of loneliness, we describe one's "subjective experience," not physical proximity to others.[2] A person feels lonely when they experience a lack of meaning or low quality in their social connection. Lonely people feel disconnected, isolated, and sometimes even alienated. It's the feeling that no one really understands you. It's the experience of having a great day but having no one to tell about it. It's the sense that no one really gets you and life would go on just the same without you.

Cacioppo and Patrick often describe the sensation of loneliness as a hunger. It's a natural, healthy impulse. We should not seek to extinguish the sensation, just as we don't silence the desires of hunger, thirst, or fatigue. Rather, we must ask important questions about how to satisfy our social needs. Cacioppo and Patrick compare the loneliness impulse to a "check engine light."[3] It's a sign that we should look under the hood. As in our cars, ignoring the light will likely lead to deeper problems in the future. We must ask honest questions about what we consider a quality, meaningful relationship and how we can enter into and keep those relationships.

In America, the highest profile warning on the seriousness of loneliness came from former Surgeon General Vivek Murty. In 2017, he began to sound the alarm on what he called the "loneliness epidemic." As the research showed the escalating rate of loneliness, he grew frustrated at the lack of attention given the issue when compared to other health risks. When pushed, Murty did not back down from the language of epidemic. "I think of loneliness as an epidemic because it affects a great number of people in our country but also because one person's loneliness can have an impact on another person. This is not a condition that is developing in isolation."[4]

Consider these statistics on the prevalence of the loneliness epidemic along with its health risks.

- The number of Americans who describe themselves as lonely has increased from 20 percent in 1980 to a 2010 rate of 40 percent.[5]

---

1. Cacioppo and Patrick, *Loneliness*, 13.
2. Cacioppo and Patrick, *Loneliness*, 5.
3. Cacioppo and Patrick, *Loneliness*, 127.
4. Mcgregor, "Ex-Surgeon General Laments."
5. Khullar, "How Social Isolation Is Killing Us."

- The number of Americans living alone has increased from 5 percent in the 1920s to a high of 27 percent in 2013.[6]

- Nearly half of respondents to a nationwide survey by health insurer Cigna say they always or sometimes feel alone, and 54 percent say they feel no one knows them well.[7]

- Chronic loneliness increases the risk of early death somewhere between 20 and 30 percent.[8]

- Chronic loneliness brings a reduction in life span similar to that of cigarette smoking and greater than that of obesity. Therefore, alleviating loneliness has the same health effect as quitting smoking or losing weight.[9]

- Chronic loneliness increases the risk of diabetes, heart disease, mental illness, cancer, depression, anxiety, mood disorders, cardiovascular impairment, chronic pain, substance abuse, Alzheimer's disease, fatigue, suicide, and the diminishment of one's immune system.[10]

- Loneliness limits creativity and impairs decision-making.[11]

- Lonely adults consume more alcohol and exercise less than non-lonely adults.[12]

Beyond these effects, loneliness looms beneath the surface of so many of our society's greatest problems. Almost weekly, we see horrific images of mass shootings. Over and over again, as information rolls out in the aftermath, we see the profile of a lonely, angry, and isolated shooter. Where I live, we regularly bemoan the cost of housing and discuss solutions for the lack of affordable housing. Yet, the number of adults living alone has reached unimagined highs. Living with family or a roommate has significant economic advantages, and yet many lack those relationships and live alone. Consider the growing lack of civility in our conversations and discourse. Slowly, we're losing the ability to talk to one another. Loneliness lies

6. Henderson, "More Americans Living Alone."

7. Chatterjee, "Americans Are a Lonely Lot."

8. Roberts, "John Cacioppo."

9. Mcgregor, "Ex-Surgeon General Laments."

10. UnLonely Project, "Not by My Selfie," https://artandhealing.org/unlonely-overview/.

11. Mcgregor, "Ex-Surgeon General Laments."

12. Cacioppo and Patrick, *Loneliness*, 30.

beneath all of these dangerous trends. For the good of everyone, we must fight this epidemic. But how?

I think back to the loss of my mother. Her absence led to a wave of loneliness in my life, which left me with crucial decisions to make. I think back to my first year at summer camp with my church in July of 1986. At this point, my mom was still alive. I had just turned eight and completed the second grade. Having heard stories from my older brother, I enthusiastically went to camp. I enjoyed the outdoors and all the games and traditions that came with camp. Not surprising, after a day or so, I felt homesick. I felt physically unwell after several days away from the familiar rhythm of home. Thankfully, I had my mother, who had come along as one of the adult helpers. When the physical sensation of needing a hug came over me, I would find her. Almost immediately, I felt well. Receiving a hug from her produced a positive physical response. I could feel it in my bones. However, she died later that August, so I did not have her hugs the next year. I still enjoyed camp overall, but I did not have the means to soothe my physical ache for a hug in the same way. Of course, I couldn't have explained this at the time, but I knew I had two choices: live with the pain of loneliness or find a way to get those hugs.

This reminds me of an episode of Shankar Vedantam's *Hidden Brain* entitled "The Lonely American Male."[13] He recounts stories of men who emphasized work and family, and yet woke up one day feeling a great absence. They nostalgically think back to days of childhood buddies, and yet their social circles get smaller and smaller as they age due to distance, busyness, and struggles to connect. I'm drawn to an excerpt of a conversation Vedantam had with Paul Kugelman concerning his search for connection.

> Vedantam: He didn't quite realize it, but his social world was shrinking. The acquaintances he made stayed acquaintances. He didn't have the time to develop these into real friendships. Family and work felt all-consuming. In his mid-40s, Paul's second marriage fell apart. His ex-wife took the kids and moved several hours away. His mother had died young, and Paul was estranged from his father. He talked to his daughter every day, but that routine ended, too. Even though he was doing meaningful work as a lawyer, it wasn't enough.
>
> Kugelman: I guess lonely's the right word. It was a very lonely time. I don't remember specific triggers. It was just the sense of absolute isolation. Absolute's too strong a word because I did go to

13. Vedantam, "Guys, We Have a Problem."

work, and I did have interactions at work, and I cherished those. But, you know, at the end of the day, it was just me.

Vedantam: He drank heavily for a while. Then he got into exercise. He eventually completed an Ironman triathlon. But these distractions couldn't quite stamp out the fact that he was desperate for friendship, for connection, so desperate that he turned to an inanimate object for comfort.

Kugelman: I was in my apartment. And one of the fixtures in the apartment was a post that runs floor to ceiling and a banister runs out of that. And the post became my friend. I would hug the post. I would hug the post for all it was worth because I was getting some kind of feedback physically. It was at that point I realized I have got to do something because when you get to the place where you need to hug a post to feel something that you need, that's—if that's not a wake-up call, nothing is.

He got so lonely and felt so isolated that he hugged a post. He didn't just hug it once; he hugged it regularly as part of his routine. When I first heard this, I grew quiet. I recognize his experience. I don't find this extraordinary. In fact, I find it rather ordinary. This is how we are. We are wired to be like this. We need connection, and when we don't find it, we search desperately for it.

When my mom wasn't there to give me hugs, I looked to find them. Of course, my dad still hugged me. But he had always been there. I needed to make up for her absence. Where did I find the hugs I needed? Where did I go to assuage my loneliness? The church. When I walked into the door of my church building, my friends' moms would hug me. Gracious, attentive women and men would teach classes about Jesus and the Bible. But more than teach, they showed Jesus to me. When they saw me, their faces brightened. They asked me specific questions about my day, listened, and then asked follow-up questions the next time I saw them. They hugged me, patted me on the head, slapped me on the back, and gave me high fives. I'm not talking about two or three people. As I pause to reflect, I can picture twenty, maybe thirty different adults who invested in me through that church during those crucial years.

In my church community, I see this frequently. We're not the most touchy-feely group of people, but we do seek to physically connect. Some, who've known each other forever, do the full hug. Many of us do the one-arm side hug. Admittedly, some just shake hands or do the shoulder pat. It's common to hear people say "I gotta get my hugs in" before and after worship. We have many who don't get hugs during the week for a variety of reasons. I've overheard several even say, "This is the only place where I get hugs." When I stand up in worship to preach, it often dawns on me: They're not just here to listen about Jesus but to see and feel Jesus. I've wondered many times: How many out there mainly come for the hugs? How many come for the touch? Could it be that hugging and shaking hands and high-fiving and fist-bumping are the most important things we do?

Medical professionals have studied this. Researchers have found that chronically lonely people have higher rates of epinephrine, a stress hormone.[14] At the same time, researchers have found that relational connections offer a rush of oxytocin.[15] Once again, loneliness is not just about our emotional state. Loneliness affects us in a physical way. Relational connection makes you healthier, just like exercise and eating right. Loneliness makes you unhealthy, just like laying around and eating a bunch of candy and chips. If you want to get healthy, it's not just about eating right and going to the gym. Social connection plays a vital role. The church has done that for me, providing me a consistent dose of oxytocin and playing a key role in my health.

I've rarely felt as lonely as I did that fall of 2000. I'd left my college buddies and girlfriend two thousand miles away. I'd left my parents and brothers one thousand miles away. I had no friends and no family anywhere close. I was lonely, and it physically hurt. Through my church, I found out about a Monday night spades group. I didn't know how to play spades, but I was desperate. I showed up at the appointed 8 p.m. time slot at the right address. The group mostly consisted of guys, and being a big sports fan, I anticipated we'd talk about that. We didn't. They enjoyed talking computers, sci-fi, and the dynamics of their work office. None of this interested me much. Yet, I went every week. Over time, I learned how to play spades, but I gotta be honest, I never learned to love spades. I went for other reasons. When I arrived, I felt isolated. As I left, I felt better, like the feel of an aspirin when you have a headache. The evening gave me a physiological rush.

About this time, I got to know the Bass family at my church. One day, the mom, Laura, told me, "Hey, I know you're lonely. If you ever just want to be around people, let us know. If you don't have plans on a Friday or Saturday night, just give us a call." I did that more than once. When you're busy and relationally connected, a free and open Saturday comes as a relief.

14. Cacioppo and Patrick, *Loneliness*, 105.
15. Cacioppo and Patrick, *Loneliness*, 140.

When isolated and lonely, a free and open Saturday can cause dread, even fear. I'd call them up. I'd drive over to their house. I joined in as they did family stuff. I watched them interact with their kids. We watched football and ate together. In just a few months, I'd gone from an active college campus to hanging out with a family I barely knew on Saturday nights. Yet, it felt so good. It kept me going. I'll never forget what they and others did for me during that time. In many ways, they saved my health.

A few years later, late on a Friday afternoon, I received a call from my friend Don, a sixty-year-old man whom we knew from church. "J.P., do you and Beth have plans tonight? I hate to be so last minute, but I can't be alone tonight. Can I take you out to dinner?" A year prior, Don's long-time wife suddenly passed away. As he faced the anniversary alone, intense loneliness set in. I'll never forget that dinner. As he told stories, we laughed, and we cried. Together, we celebrated that no matter what happens, we're not alone. We have each other. After talking for hours, we slowly walked to our cars in the restaurant parking lot. As we said goodbye, he thanked us. We thanked him. And then, he gave me a big bear hug. We looked at each and smiled. We're not alone.

6

Churchless Christianity

I'VE ALWAYS ENJOYED THE Indiana Jones movies, but I gravitate most to the 1989 *Indiana Jones and the Last Crusade*. The inclusion of Sean Connery as the father of Indiana Jones, Harrison Ford, cements this as my favorite. I love their father-and-son banter throughout the film. Specifically, I like how the father always refers to his son as "Junior" while the son always complains with a response of "Call me Indiana." It provides some comic relief throughout the action scenes. However, at the climactic scene, as they struggle to find and rescue the Holy Grail, danger surrounds the son. He's hanging off a ledge. His father, safely on top of the ledge, grabs one hand, yet the son stubbornly twists and turns while reaching for the Holy Grail with his other hand. Gradually, he slips more and more from his father's grasp. "Give me your other hand," the father repeats. Finally, with all the gravitas one expects from a Sean Connery line, the father says, "Indiana, give me your other hand." Hearing his desired name, the son pauses, turns, and gives him his other hand. He loses the Holy Grail, but he saves his life. I love that scene.

At birth, my parents named me Joseph Paul. My first name comes from Joseph in the Old Testament, who endured brutal betrayal, enslavement, and imprisonment before rising to prominence in Egypt. He developed a food storage plan in the face of a future famine that ultimately saved the very brothers that betrayed him. My middle name comes from Paul in the New Testament, who went from persecuting Christians to becoming a persecuted Christian after experiencing a vision on the road to Damascus.

I love my name, and in times of wrestling with my identity I've gone back to the stories of my namesakes.

Growing up, though, everyone called me Joe Paul. In the South, double names were not uncommon. I always liked my name. Yet, as I grew closer to leaving for college, I became excited about a fresh start. At that age, moving to a place where no one knew me sounded refreshing. I realized the great opportunity to reinvent myself, to continue my strengths but minimize or even leave behind my weaknesses. As a sign of this, when I set foot on my college campus I introduced myself as "J.P." Ever since, I've gone by that name. Even though I live now not far from where I grew up, most everyone calls me J.P. Most of the people I interact with did not know me as a child.

But some still call me Joe Paul. My parents call me that. My brothers call me that. If I'm ever out and about and hear the name Joe Paul, I immediately stop. I know I'm encountering someone who knew me as a child or teenager. When I hear the name, I instantly know that we go way back. There's a history and depth that comes with the name. My best friends, the ones I've known my whole life and continue to share life with, mostly call me J.P. But on occasion, they call me Joe Paul. It normally happens when the conversation gets serious. It normally happens around things that truly matter. I can remember more than one occasion when I contemplated a big decision. I needed advice. I wanted to talk to someone who calls me Joe Paul, who has known me forever.

Two of those friends are Travis and Todd. I never remember meeting them. For as long as I can remember, they have been there. Likely, our first introduction came in a church nursery. Growing up, we participated in church together multiple times a week. Over the course of our childhood and adolescence, I sat beside them in well over a thousand worship services and Bible classes. After high school graduation, we drove to California and back from Tennessee, over four thousand miles in twelve days. Through car trouble in the Mojave Desert, a full moon in Yosemite, and a sunrise over the Grand Canyon, they were there. When I buried my mother, they were there. When I got baptized, they were there. When I got married, they were there. When I go through really hard, even embarrassing times, they are there. Even though we don't live in the same state or participate in the same congregation, they were and still are church to me.

When I hear my real name, I feel truly known. For me, this has led to the following realization. Besides family, the people who truly know me are people who have participated in church with me. This forms the backdrop of the question that must be faced. It's impossible to have an honest reflection on church without addressing the question that lingers in the background. Do I have to have a church? Is it necessary? What's the point?

For many, the answer to these questions shows up this way. To be a Christian means you attend church and refrain from, or at least hide, involvement in a few socially unacceptable sins. The best way to measure a successful Christian life is how someone looks between nine and eleven on Sunday morning. If you show up for God and avoid the big sins, you're good with the Almighty. Life transformation doesn't really show up in the answer. Understandably, many have found this answer shallow, even harmful. I agree. I have found this approach wanting, even destructive at times.

We need a better framework for understanding the purpose of church and specifically what it means to be a disciple of Jesus. In 1998, Dallas Willard published his work *The Divine Conspiracy*. In it, he popularized the notion of the "gospel of sin management."[1] In this paradigm, Christians assess the success of their faith on their ability to manage temptation. Whether it be gambling or pornography or gossip, discipleship focuses on limiting their sin to occasional struggles versus frequent falls. In many ways, they see following Jesus like a batting average in baseball. No one is perfect, but if I can keep my average or score at a certain level, I can feel good about my walk with Christ. As Willard artfully points out, it's a rather limiting way to look at kingdom life. It's an inherently negative and cynical way to approach life, letting sin set the agenda instead of the joy of walking with Jesus. It's a pursuit of resisting wrong rather than embracing good, as well as the practices which produce goodness. It's a faith practice that talks more about what we're against than about what we're for.

I found his description compelling and immediately saw the "gospel of sin management" as the dominant discipleship model around me. Within this paradigm, church attendance shows up as a huge plank. While I've rarely heard skipping church proclaimed as a sin, it's normally implied through numerous indirect means. If you want to resist sin, you better be in church on Sunday. If you're having trouble resisting sin, it's probably because you weren't at church. If you were at church, perhaps consider attending more and more of the church's ministries, gatherings, and programs. Sin is the problem, and attendance is the solution.

This posture misses the point of Jesus' teaching. Christ did not come for people to attend his meetings. Christ did not come for people

---

1. Willard, *Divine Conspiracy*, 41.

to consume his programs. Jesus came so that we could become more like him. Jesus taught so the student could become like the teacher. Jesus came to save us, so we could live the healthy life we were always intended to live. The point was a group of people that look and live like Jesus, not just a group of people sitting in pews on Sunday. It's not about attendance and consumption but about participation and engagement.

I want to be honest about what I have seen. At most every church I have been around, I have known people who attended but had no interest in becoming like Jesus. They had been baptized into the "gospel of sin management." Because they went to church and stayed away from that short list of socially unacceptable sins, they hoped to go to heaven someday. But, they had little interest in heaven today. They had no interest in a sacrificial life of loving their neighbor and living out the fruit of the Spirit. If you've been turned off by that, know this: I agree with you. I have zero interest in church attendance based on rigid rules, guilty feelings, or shoddy theology.

Still, as I've looked for Christians who really live as imitations of Christ, in most every case they have a consistent relationship with a group of Christians. Solid disciples of Jesus normally have a support group for encouragement and collaboration. They don't view church as a box to check but a group to facilitate their formation into Christ. Community matters. For this reason, I'm not certain churchless Christians will find what they're really looking for. I wonder if pursuing Jesus solely outside the church offers a sustainable model of experiencing Jesus.

Let me step back for a second. Perhaps some terminology is helpful. As previously noted, the number of Americans who identify as having no religion at all has steadily climbed in recent decades. Currently, it hovers around 20 percent. Often, sociologists and researchers refer to this group as the "Nones." This group has received ample research over the last decade. Some identify as atheists and some as agnostics. Some would say they are "spiritual but not religious."

In addition, I find a second group equally as interesting. Sociologists have identified a group that continues to self-identity as Christian and yet no longer identifies as a church member. Currently, this group hovers around 10 percent of the American population.[2] Researchers have begun to describe this group as the "Dones." They have not attended a church gathering in the past sixth months. Still, they maintain many of the core Christian beliefs. Most all of them believe in one all-powerful and all-knowing God

2. Barna Group, "Meet Those Who 'Love Jesus.'"

who created the world. They pray at the same rate as churchgoing Christians. If you talked to them about faith, you'd find considerable agreement between them and churchgoing Christians.

Now, as we explore the churchless faith of the "Dones," it's important to be specific. I'm not talking about Christians who worship in house churches or other nontraditional expressions. I'm not talking about my Christians friends who've left "organized church" but host open weekly gatherings with Christians for dinner and a Scripture reading. I'm not talking about new monastics and communal living groups that regularly meet together in the context of their lifestyle. In a broad sense, any group of disciples that makes a commitment to gather regularly to lift up Christ and encourage each other in discipleship represents a church. Since the Greek word translated as church, *ekklesia*, literally means "assembly" or "meeting," any group that meets or assembles in the name of Christ is a church. Do some disagree with that definition? Sure. Honestly, there's so much more I want to add to the definition, but I stop myself. I want to work with that lowest common denominator understanding to set the stage. If we disagree on forms of meetings, that's a conversation among church Christians. If we disagree on whether we should meet, that's a conversation between church and churchless Christians.

How did they end up here? There doesn't appear to be one main reason that leads one to cease church affiliation and practice. I've seen at least seven reasons, ranging in significance and prevalence. First, many leave because of bad experiences. Much of this came up in the focus on brokenness. Mistreatment, ranging from abuse to gossip, has left many saying, "No thanks." I've listened to so many share the pain. They just can't go back. They opened themselves up to the church. They made themselves vulnerable only to be wounded, leaving a deep pain. These disappointments built over time. I've listened to more than one friend basically say, "When it happened at one church, I got over it. When it happened at two to three churches in a row, I figured it was easier to follow Jesus without the church."

Second, I know many who have ventured into a churchless state of faith as they encountered new religious ideas. Ranging from how to view the Bible to experiences with other religions to a transition to another doctrinal position, their current church does not fit well with their new beliefs. In fact, often they perceive incompatibility, even hostility, between their church and new ideas. Normally, this shows up in a progression from traditional views to progressive views, but I've also seen it happen as someone shifts to a more traditional view. Prevalent issues in this category include politics, gender, sexuality, race, science, and economics. In these circumstances, many step away from church to get their bearings. Eventually, some in this category will find a church that fits better with their new views.

Third, some leave church due to social complications. In recent years, I've encountered a growing number of believers who experience social anxiety, even panic attacks, around attending a church gathering. For some, the stress of opening that door and finding someone to talk to proves too challenging. Admittedly, for someone going alone to a new gathering, church brings enormous social risk. Where will I sit? Will anyone talk to me? What will we talk about? Anxiety of the social unknown can paralyze.

Fourth, the busyness of modern life slowly moves many away from church practice. Contemporary Americans live life at a frenetic pace. We work hard and play hard. For busy people, if church involvement becomes optional, it can easily become obsolete. Just the other day, I had lunch with Dan, a friend in his twenties. He deeply loves the Lord and lives a life of self-sacrifice. Yet, he frantically jumps from activity to activity with little consistency. He's kind and sincere, but not rooted. I confess I experience much of this in my own life. At times, my schedule seems to have a mind of its own. I feel out of control in my commitments. I do a lot, but I'm not sure I do anything well. I feel like I float, instead of live.

Fifth, the demands of family responsibility can prove disruptive to normal life patterns, including church involvement. When someone experiences the addition of a child, it normally shapes their family rhythm, work life, and hobbies. It makes sense that the addition of children will affect church life as well. At my congregation, we like to quote Mrs. Dot, one of the matriarchs of our community, who raised three boys. She likes to describe the challenge of getting kids to and through church in this manner. "Some Sundays I lost more religion than I gained." For sure, it can be a lot.

Sixth, many come to the point where they believe the time spent with church can be better used elsewhere. In some ways, this connects with the busyness of modern life yet goes beyond it. Many of us have experienced an internally focused church that bordered on self-absorption. I've listened to many who basically said, "I was spending all this time with my church, but we weren't serving our neighbors. I didn't have time to do both, so I decided to devote those two to three hours a week to volunteering in the community." Sadly, for many churches, involvement leads to detachment from the world and away from neighbor engagement. I affirm these instincts but long to see this channeled towards the reform of the church.

Seventh, more than one friend has just departed over apathy. They just wake up one day and realize they don't care anymore. Maybe it's boredom. Maybe it's a growing sense of the irrelevancy of many church conversations. One student told me this about her and her husband. "We left for a couple of months and realized our lives didn't change. We still helped others. We still gave money to the poor. We still loved God. When nothing changed, we decided that going to church didn't make a difference. We haven't gone back."

I'm guessing that you have stories around at least some of these seven options. I'm even guessing that you could add additional categories. There's no one reason why people leave church. It happens for all sorts of reasons. The link between all the reasons is this. They decide that church is not worth it. So why does it matter? Why am I drawn to this group of sisters and brothers in Christ?

Churchless Christianity rarely exists as a permanent state for a believer. In the long run, it's unsustainable. In many ways, it's a way station between belief and unbelief. I believe that most who enter a churchless stage of faith will eventually leave Christianity or get back into church. Simply put, most "Dones" will become "Nones" if they don't reenter the communal Christian practices of church. Consider the trends seen in "Dones" from the Barna research. About half believe that all religions basically teach the same thing. They talk about spiritual matters with friends at half the rate of churchgoing believers. Likewise, they believe Christians have a responsibility to evangelize at half the rate of churchgoers. Finally, in similar fashion, they read their Bibles at less than half the rate of churchgoing Christians. Together, this paints the picture of a believer shifting away from orthodox Christianity, not towards it.

If this is you, let me put my cards on the table. I miss you. There's more. We miss your gifts. We miss your creativity and contributions. You made our churches better. While you may have found a type of community elsewhere, many have not. Your consistent presence enabled us to better welcome them. We want you back. I'm sorry for your pain. I sympathize with your reasons. You're not wrong. But let me be honest. I don't think this current path will bring you what you desire. I don't think churchless Christianity represents the most vibrant expression of the gospel.

While broken, the church offers a beauty that cannot be experienced elsewhere. In section 2, I want to consider that beauty. No other social group can give us what the church gives us. Community matters, and I believe no community offers as much consistent, rooted community as church.

If you've been hurt, I'm sorry. If you need time to heal, I pray in time you'll find that healing. Take your time. If your new understanding of faith doesn't fit your former community, find a new church community that does. I don't say that to minimize theological convictions. I simply would rather see people become a part of a church, even if I might personally have some disagreements with it, than not be a part of any church. We were created with a heart that seeks after our Creator, and we were created with hearts that need each other. I believe church communities are worth it.

One Sunday morning, during the first semester of my freshman year of college, miles away from my family, I didn't get out of bed. I just laid there and said, "I'm not gonna do it this morning." For the first time, I skipped. To be clear, I'd missed plenty of Sundays for sickness and traveling. Yet, this was the first time in my life that I was on my own, could have gone, and decided not to. I slept in an extra hour, and then drove my roommate's car to a nearby lake. I read and enjoyed the quiet. It was a decent day. It wasn't the only time during college that I did this. Part of me enjoyed the solo time on those Sundays, but they felt a tad hollow. Nothing really happened. Even now, when I miss meeting with the church on Sunday, I feel a void. I miss my people. True, God doesn't strike us dead or love us less if we miss. Yet, I've found my life is better with church than without church.

I used to ask, "Do I have to go to church?" I quit asking that because I've come to realize this for me. I have to. I need to. I want to. Why? Because I long for a people that know my name. I long for people who call me Joe Paul. I long to be known and to be loved. I long for a group of people to do life with. And a mysterious thing happens. When I'm surrounded by a group that truly knows me in my inadequacy and still loves me, I'm reminded that God does as well. When I'm surrounded by people that call my name, I'm able to hear the voice of the God who calls me, who named me, and who continues to speak. I don't want to miss any of that.

SECTION 2

Beautiful

7

Kingdom

Tasting Heaven on Earth

ITALY HOLDS A SPECIAL place for my family. My wife, Beth, was born there and lived there until age four. Her parents hold numerous friendships with Italians and travel there regularly. In 2006, before we had children, Beth and I traveled there for the first time with them. One day, they took me to Venice, a city where they had all been many times. You may have been to this one-of-a-kind city of waterways and gondolas without cars. As we began to walk the city, I felt overwhelmed as if transported to a distant reality. Normally, I talk a lot, but I couldn't figure out what to say. No words could describe the beauty, design, and uniqueness. "What do you think?" they kept asking me. I didn't know what to say. Finally, I blurted out, "It's so amazing, like no place I've ever been. It's incredible, like Epcot." Immediately, the three of them stopped. "Epcot?" they asked. Ah, I knew I had made a mistake. They responded, "Epcot? No, no. Venice is not like Epcot. Oh no. Epcot is an attempt to be like Venice. Epcot is great, but it's an imitation. This is the real thing."

When I was six, my family went on a trip to Disney World. One day, we walked all over Epcot. We spent hours visiting all the country displays with their exhibits and restaurants. They offer a taste, a glimpse, of life in a far-off place. As a kid, it all felt so magical. For years, I held on to this memory. It held such a power over me that when I got to the real thing, the real Venice, I didn't know what to do. Imitation distracted me from reality.

When it comes to the church, we have done the same thing. We have forgotten the reality and settled for the imitation. The kingdom of God is the real thing. The church on earth is the imitation. Of course, it's an inspired imitation, but because of human sin, it will never offer a complete kingdom experience. The kingdom is Venice. The church is Epcot. Think about it. Epcot is good, even great, but it only holds magic because it reminds you of the real Venice. The church only has power when it resembles the kingdom. If there is anything good about the church (and there is much), it's because of its connection to the kingdom. Sadly though, we can get so accustomed to the church on earth that we don't know what to do with the kingdom.

Allow me to back up a second. Think for a moment on this question. Why did Jesus come to earth? To save us. That's the normal answer, and yes, it's correct. But what is salvation? Reflect on this for a minute. Jesus said in John 10:10, "I have come that they might have life and have it to the full." Jesus came that we might live full lives. Jesus came so that we could live the life God always intended for us. It's a long, eternal life as well as a healthy, good life. It offers endless quantity and utmost quality. To experience this life is to know the will of God, and the will of God is the kingdom.

I like how Dallas Willard describes it. Willard says the kingdom is "the realm of God's effective will."[1] It is the area where what God wants to happen actually happens. It centers on total peace as God has designed. It's "effective" in that God causes and supports it. This "will" comes from God and exists for God's glory. Jesus references it in the famous Lord's Prayer. "Your kingdom come, your will be done, on earth as it is in heaven." This is why Jesus came. Jesus came for us to truly live.

As a kid, if you had asked me what it meant to truly live, I had an answer for you. To me, it didn't get any better than an ice cream social in the summer. Growing up in the South, after a day of sweating, I loved the soothing comfort of cold ice cream. More than that, I loved the abundance of an ice cream social. My parents, to their credit, regulated my portions when at home. However, at a big party no one kept track of how much I ate. A summer ice cream social equals abundant comfort. Specifically, I've always had a thing for homemade peach ice cream, especially when the peaches hit their perfect ripeness.

Besides the occasional family or friend ice cream gathering, our church always had a big ice cream social once every summer. Our church consisted of rich, poor, and middle class, but no matter your situation, we

---

1. Willard, *Divine Conspiracy*, 25.

had plenty of ice cream for everyone. One of our church leaders owned a dairy which had begun to make their own ice cream. On this annual summer night, he brought a large amount of multiple flavors of their ice cream. Often, I had up to six to seven servings of ice cream on these nights. I liked to refer to it as the night we had ice cream and nothing but ice cream for dinner. We roped off the church parking lot, and my buddies and I would run all over, physically enhanced by the sugar rush. We'd watch the sunset and grab one more serving. Eventually, our families would tell us it was time to go home. At this age, I couldn't spell utopia or understand heaven, yet this was it.

This is why Jesus came to earth. I'm serious. While he didn't come for ice cream socials, he came to bring us life. Jesus came to give a taste and glimpse of heaven even for us still on earth. I believe in resurrection. I believe we will live in the new heavens and new earth someday, but I also believe Jesus wants to give us some heaven now. Why else would he pray for the kingdom to come now? His followers definitely wanted that glimpse. As we read the story of Jesus now, many of us may feel satisfied after the crucifixion and resurrection. The disciples were not. Even after the resurrection, they wanted more. In Acts 1:6, they asked him, "Lord are you at this time going to restore the kingdom to Israel?" They grew up anticipating a coming king. They had turned their lives upside down to follow Jesus as king. They weren't content with the story up to this point. They wanted a kingdom. Jesus answers by telling them they will receive the Holy Spirit and become witnesses of Christ. In other words, the kingdom will come, and they will be part of it. In the next chapter of Acts, we see the story of Pentecost and the birth of the church.

The church is the social expression of the kingdom. Disciples are the citizens of the kingdom, the people of the Jesus movement. Jesus sent down the Spirit to give us the power to truly live according to his will, to be people that reflect the kingdom. Everything that is good about the church comes only to the degree that it resembles the kingdom. Everything that is good about the church comes only by the power of the Spirit. Everything that is good about church comes through its resemblance to the original, Jesus.

Think of it this way. Early on in Jesus' ministry, John the Baptist sends his disciples to see if Jesus is in fact the real deal, the long-anticipated king. We read this in Luke 7:21-22.

> At that very time Jesus cured many who had diseases, sicknesses and evil spirits, and gave sight to many who were blind. So he

replied to the messengers, "Go back and report to John what you have seen and heard: The blind receive sight, the lame walk, those who have leprosy are cleansed, the deaf hear, the dead are raised, and the good news is proclaimed to the poor."

Jesus doesn't give a simple yes or no, but rather, he asks them what they see. Clearly, they see the kingdom at work. This is the heart of the Jesus movement, the original kingdom. Notice the similarity between this and the church in Acts 2:42–47, right after the Pentecost experience.

> They devoted themselves to the apostles' teaching and to fellowship, to the breaking of bread and to prayer. Everyone was filled with awe at the many wonders and signs performed by the apostles. All the believers were together and had everything in common. They sold property and possessions to give to anyone who had need. Every day they continued to meet together in the temple courts. They broke bread in their homes and ate together with glad and sincere hearts, praising God and enjoying the favor of all the people. And the Lord added to their number daily those who were being saved.

The church is the social experience of the kingdom. Church should imitate the kingdom, the original.

I grew up among congregations known as Churches of Christ. Even today, I still serve in this movement. Like any expression of church, we've had our struggles, but I've always been drawn to this emphasis. We read Acts a lot. We talk about Acts a lot. A deep desire to experience the kingdom together through church unites us. I grew up on the vision of being a kingdom community, and I'm still drawn to it. I'm a hopeless romantic for it. Even though I've been let down at times, I haven't given up, because so many times over the years I got a taste of it. So often, my experience with church has looked like Jesus, just as Acts 2 resembles Luke 7. Church potlucks. Ice cream socials. Canned food drives. Helping strangers who came in off the street. Loving a kid who just lost his mom. It all felt like the life Jesus wanted for us. From my earliest days, I fell in love with Jesus, and because the church was like Jesus, I fell in love with the church.

Did it always live up to this? Of course not. The church on earth is Epcot. It's good, even great, but as long as humans mess up, it will never be Venice. I compare it to an awkward family photo. Do you have those? My parents still have one hanging on their living room wall. Around age eleven, I decided I wanted a flat-top haircut. Several of my buddies had one. Spiked hair was in style. Fresh out of the barber shop, it looked good. But if too many weeks went by, it got a little wild. Honestly, I'm not sure I was cool enough to pull it off. Part of me wants to forget that hairstyle, but every time I go to my parent's house, a reminder remains on the wall. It's an awkward photo. We all have one. When I see it now, I just shrug my shoulders. I know the look I was going for. I did my best, even if it looks awkward now.

The church exists in a perpetual awkward stage. Until Jesus returns, we will never get it all right. We'll never completely embrace and live out the kingdom. This helps me process the times the church falls short of the kingdom while not letting go of the kingdom vision. Our churches are not perfect, but they weren't perfect in the days of Acts either. A quick glance of the New Testament shows backstabbing, gossip, divisions, and rancor. The church has never completely resembled the kingdom. We've always been awkward.

Even at those wondrous ice cream socials, I remember things that could have been better, much better. Among us kids, I remember teasing. I remember kids getting left out. I confess I was not always on the right side of this. In many ways, it was so perfect. In many ways, it was not. When I run into old friends from those days, it's interesting to see what people re- member. Some mostly hold on to the beauty and wonder of the community and the divine transcendence behind it all. Like me, most of these continue some type of engagement with local churches. Some mostly hold on to the dysfunction, lack of flexibility on traditions, and judgmental tones. For the most part, they don't participate with church anymore. It's too painful.

I understand their feelings and perspective, and I'm sorry. But, I have good news. Their negative experiences are not indicative of the kingdom. The greatest negative of closely associating the kingdom with the church centers on the kingdom getting blamed for the sin of the church. There will always be a slice of the church that represents the kingdom, just as there will always be a slice that doesn't. For those who have left, for those churchless Christians, we can say, "We know. We're sorry. That was not the kingdom. Yes, the church disappointed you, but the kingdom never will."

In the here and now, until Jesus comes, what should we do? I'm advo- cating, like many before me in history, the pursuit of the perfect kingdom through the means of a currently imperfect church. In doing so, we must admit when the church does not resemble the kingdom without letting cynicism steal our thirst for the life Jesus wants for us. We can look people in the eye and accurately say, "The brokenness you experience in church and religion was not the kingdom. That wasn't Jesus. There is something out there better." In this way, we're not asking people to give the church a second chance as much as we're asking someone to give the kingdom a second chance. We don't believe the church is perfect. We just think it's the best way to glimpse that which is perfect. And those glimpses keep me coming back.

I loved those ice cream socials. In fact, as I write this, my church had one just last night. We went to the local park down the street from our church building. We had a mix of homemade and store-bought ice cream, along with some popsicles. The kids ran back and forth between the playground and second helpings of ice cream. The adults sought shade in the midst of a sweltering late June Southern melt. Some recent additions to our church family came out, and we enjoyed getting to know them better. Several had expressed the complications of finding a church family. A group of women sat around communicating through sign language. Some brought new friends we'd never met. One person bent my ear about an organization that fights human trafficking. We discussed ways for our church to fight alongside them. In many ways, nothing about the evening seemed innovative or earth shattering. Still, the lonely found friends. The comfortable got stretched. We talked about ways to expand the kingdom, the realm where what God wants to happen actually happens. It was nothing extravagant, yet I'd call it a good night. More than that, I'd call it a glimpse of the kingdom. This is what church offers. The church brings a social pursuit of the kingdom which chips away at the brokenness of the world.

It reminds me of my favorite ice cream social moment. Looking back, I was probably around ten years old, and my mom had been gone for about two years. At first, I couldn't stomach the idea of my father remarrying. It felt disloyal. Yet, by this point, I longed for another mother. My dad performed admirably under the circumstances, but I longed to have a woman in the house. I didn't want a replacement for my mother, but I did want a mother. On this night, my dad talked for a long time with the man who ran the dairy. Dad seemed focused on the conversation, and with my well-developed eavesdropping skills, I gathered the conversation centered on dating. Later, Dad filled me in. The gentleman told him, "I'm not sure if you have any interest in dating. But if you do, I want you to know I have a list of ten single Christian women in Nashville for you." (I don't think he had a written list. It was just his jovial way of saying he had a few women in mind.) "Well," my dad responded with a smile. "I guess we should start with the first one." He then proceeded to tell him about the woman who became and remains my second mother. The church not only stepped in as my mother, the church gave me another mother. God used her at a key time in my life to mend some of the brokenness. It didn't fix all the past. It wasn't the way any of us would have written the story, yet God used her to bring some beauty to my life that was lacking.

So, I like ice cream socials. None had a greater impact on my life than that one. It gave me a glimpse of the kingdom, the way life should be. The church offered a beauty that overwhelmed the brokenness. I love the kingdom, and when the church reflects the kingdom, it's really good, even great. I don't love Venice because it's like Epcot. I love Epcot because it's like Venice.

8

Resilient Exiles

PERHAPS THE MOST BEAUTIFUL church I've ever experienced was also the most broken. One Good Friday, the church discovered one of their leaders in a secret, inappropriate relationship. When confronted, he simply packed up and left, promptly leaving behind his wife and children to live with a young, single woman. The news of this revelation sent a wave of devastation through the church. That Friday night, many in the church met to grieve. They assembled at one house to process their shock and console each other. They wept. How did this happen? Why hadn't they seen it coming? What might they have done to prevent it? What would they do now? How would this shape how the community viewed their congregation? They felt pain. They felt anger. They felt embarrassment. They felt broken.

Despite their grief, on that Sunday, Easter Sunday, the church met to worship. To be clear, many did not feel like worshipping. They didn't assemble because of happiness. You might say they met out of desperation. They met to confess the gospel of Jesus. Christ has come. Christ has risen. Christ will come again. They proclaimed what they did not yet experience. In the midst of their pain, Jesus did not seem risen. They did not experience the joy of an empty tomb, but rather the smell of death surrounded them. Still, they met. They greeted each other. They sang, prayed, and read the Scriptures. The grieving preacher gave his best Easter sermon. The grieving church, including devasted family members and friends, listened with open hearts. Then, the service climaxed with the Lord's Table. They broke the beautiful body of Jesus and ate it. For in the broken and beautiful body, they hoped to find life. This is what resilience looks like.

I began serving as the youth minister at this congregation four months later. I lived among them for over six years. During my tenure, I coordinated spiritual education, service learning, and social connection for the fifty-plus middle and high school students connected with this three-hundred-member congregation. My time with them galvanized my resolve that church is truly worth it, but it was all far from easy.

I arrived at this congregation on September 1, 2000, after driving alone two previous days. I'd left both the house of my youth as well as the town of my college years. A fear of the unknown mixed with a hopeful curiosity. After all, I was trained for this. I'd completed an undergraduate degree in ministry and completed multiple summer internships. I was ready, or so I thought. Passionate about the Lord, I'd longed for this day to enter into the exciting life of a minister. I'll never forget my first day. I stopped by the church office to begin organizing my office. As it turned out, the preacher had a week-long vacation scheduled the following day, so he took me out for a coffee to chat at Dunkin Donuts. This became a consistent pattern for us. He's one of the kindest, most gracious people I've ever known, and he quickly became a valued mentor of mine.

Already, I was well aware of the high-profile incident of the spring. Through various phone conversations over the summer, I'd become convinced they'd taken important steps towards healing and reconciliation. In my youthful optimism, I assumed these broken stories were few and far between. They were not and are not. Because of this, his conversation caught me off guard. Confidentially, he wanted me to know of another potential family break up on the horizon. Absent of gossip and full of concern, he calmly told me of some behind the scenes struggles among families in our congregation. As I looked out on the ocean of the future, more and more waves were coming. Looking back now, I recognize my own naïveté at the time, but this left me speechless. I assumed that brokenness would be an every-now-and-then occurrence. Instead, brokenness would be a persistent, daily reality.

Why does the church feel so broken? Why is it so hard? I never expected it to be like this. Obviously, I shouldn't have been surprised. I'd seen plenty of brokenness throughout my life. Moreover, I had plenty of it in my own life. We're all sinners. We all struggle. None of us live perfect lives, and as we make up groups, our involvement ensures their imperfection.

Still, the persistent reality of harsh difficulties in this new church family left me with a profound sense of disorientation. I felt a deep sense of distance from what I sensed life should be. I had trouble explaining what I felt until I encountered a neglected biblical category.

Around this time, some gifted teachers took me back to this part of the Bible and showed me the biblical category of exile. My life and outlook have never been the same. In the late seventh and early sixth centuries B.C., the Israelites went into Babylonian captivity. After years of failing to heed the prophet's warning over their mistreatment of the marginalized as well as their idol worship, they found themselves in exile. They were the quintessential "strangers in a strange land." Many slowly blended into Babylonian society. However, a remnant persisted in their Jewish and monotheistic identity despite not being anywhere near the temple. The exilic life involves a considerable amount of resilience and resolve. You live like home is real even while you're far from home. Later, even though some went back to Jerusalem, the exile experience proved a template for their ensuing occupations by other world powers, eventually including Roman occupation during the life of Jesus.

The Bible offers many writings from this time period, but my favorite quote comes from the first lines of Psalm 137.

> By the rivers of Babylon we sat and wept when we remembered Zion. There on the poplars we hung our harps, for there our captors asked us for songs, our tormentors demanded songs of joy; they said, "Sing us one of the songs of Zion!" How can we sing the songs of the Lord while in a foreign land?

While certainly not to the depths of their experience, I felt a profound disorientation because life is simply not as it should be. To borrow a phrase from John Steinbeck, I felt "east of Eden."[1] I longed to experience life as God created it to be away from this tragic fallenness. I longed for heaven but too much of life felt like hell. How could I sing songs of joy on Sunday morning when families experienced so much pain? How could I plan lessons on the Bible when so many experienced drug addiction, abuse, and cancer?

How do you live a life of faith, hope, and love in the midst of exile? I think back to that Good Friday in 2000. How do you gather to sing songs of worship when you feel like your world is falling apart? As I got to know them, I realized how. Due to licensing requirements, our worship leader

---

1. Steinbeck, *East of Eden*.

kept track of which songs we sang and how often we sang them. My first
year there, the number one song was not "Amazing Grace" or other classics
such as "Nothing but the Blood" or "How Great Thou Art." The number one
song was not any of the new praise and worship songs of that era. Instead,
the most frequent song in worship was the late nineteenth-century hymn
"I Am Resolved."

As I lived among this broken church, a sense of resolve appeared to
be the most faithful response to the profound sense of loss. They channeled
an exilic identity. Things were not as they should be, and yet we needed to
press on. That's what I saw in those around me. It was not a perfect church,
and I was not a perfect minister. Yet, we consistently gathered out of faithful
commitment to God and each other. In this resolute attitude, this spiritual
stubbornness, I found reorientation in the midst of disorientation. I experienced a type of joy and camaraderie that rose above our circumstances.

In exile, you have two options: resilience or death—if not literal death
then at least death of identity. To be a church of resilient exiles simply means
this. We don't claim to have it all together. We don't claim to be perfect. We
confess brokenness, the sins we commit as well as the inexplicable challenges of this fallen world. But, we refuse to give into cynicism and despair.
We cling to the kingdom, even if it seems far off, even elusive. Life doesn't
feel like heaven, yet we're heaven people. It's gutsy to embrace the reality of
heaven in a world that often seems like hell on earth.

Over and over, I've found strength in the biblical stories of exile,
especially the lives of Daniel and Esther. When Daniel found himself
presented with a new royal Babylonian diet, he stuck to his diet. In the
end, it worked better, and all could see. When Daniel's friends got asked
to bow down to the statue, they resisted. Later, when Daniel heard of a
law against prayer, he went straight home and broke the law. When they
threw him in the lion's den, God rescued him. Each time, Daniel persisted
in living like he's still in Israel. Each time, Daniel resisted letting his sur-
roundings change his outlook.

We find similar power in the story of Esther. Under exile, this time to
Persia, the Hebrews continued to seek faithfulness. Despite being married
to King Xerxes, she seemingly had little influence. Yet, when the villain-
ous Haman wanted to exterminate the Hebrew people, she found her voice
and power. She stood up to Xerxes and ruined Haman's plot. Jews continue
to celebrate this reprieve in the feast of Purim. Daniel never went back to
Israel. Esther never lived in Israel. Yet both lived for the God of Israel in a

foreign land. They were heaven people in hellacious circumstances. They were kingdom citizens in the midst of exile to foreign powers. They exercised stubborn resolve in the midst of great disorientation, and through that they maintained their identity and found their way. This is what resilience looks like.

What does this look like for us? In February of 2006, I took a group of teenagers from this church to a large out-of-state youth conference. We looked forward to this all year. We loved all the stories and memories that came from the van ride and time in the hotel. We longed for the spiritual encouragement of the worship. For most of them, they'd never seen so many Christian teens gathered in one spot. Every year we went, it proved inspirational. It gave us a glimpse of the beauty of the kingdom.

But this particular year, we got a glimpse of the brokenness as well. During one of the breaks in the conference, many of the teens went shopping. After a while, my phone rang. One of our girls had been picked up for shoplifting. As you can imagine, this arrest caused quite the scare and panic among the teens. I still remember driving to the jail. I remember calling her parents and getting her out. She was so embarrassed, even humiliated. Her parents were embarrassed, even angry. I desperately assured her that we loved her. This incident would not have the final word. I assured her that this one-time decision did not define her. When we got back to the group, we huddled everyone together. We reminded each other of the unconditional love and forgiveness of Jesus. Still, it all felt so heavy.

As you can imagine, news of this swept the congregation as all the parents found out about it. There was more. Two weeks after the trip, one of the teen boys got picked up with drug paraphernalia. When his parents asked him where he got it, he confessed he got it on our trip. Eventually, I learned more. On the night before the trip, several teenage boys stayed over at one house to make departure easier. That night, they walked down the street and smoked marijuana together.

Within a few days, we held the best-attended parents meeting I ever held in my ten years as a youth minister. I think we almost achieved 100 percent attendance. Certainly, many harbored great concern and suspicion. Some wondered if the negatives of spending time with these "church teens" outweighed the positives. "What are these kids doing to my kids? Can I trust sending them with you? Are you teaching them anything?" In the midst of it all, I tried to talk about Jesus' call to holiness alongside Jesus' affirmation of grace and love. While some wanted to make rules, more wanted to win hearts. Looking back now, I see it as one of the more stressful moments of my life. I wanted them to know they were loved. At the same time, I wanted them to have a greater sense of what God wanted for their lives. We felt like exiles, but we longed for the kingdom.

Around this same time, one of the older women in our congregation gave me a call. For years, she'd been the primary guardian for her grandson. Despite deep poverty, she courageously fought to raise him well and keep him from going down the wrong path. She struggled to pay the bills at times, but he always had necessities. He regularly participated in our ministry. So, when his school principal called her about some trouble with him, she called me. As it turns out, he'd been having sexually graphic conversations at the lunch table. The conversations ventured into notes, which got turned into the teacher. When the grandmother and I read them, we knew some of the content exceeded his imagination. There must be a source. She called me over to the house, and we talked kindly but firmly to the young man. He apologized for the notes but denied having any graphic content. These were the days before everyone had a phone with the Internet. Going on instinct, I walked into his room and lifted his mattress. Immediately, a pornographic magazine fell out. His face fell. An intense pain of disappointment and fear came across her face. His grandmother asked him to get it all out right then, and he responded by pulling out multiple magazines from multiple hiding spots. I told him it was gonna be okay. This stuff just wasn't good for him. I told him that I'd seen stuff which I wish I'd never seen. I gave him a hug. Then, his grandmother had him sit down and page by page shred every part of every magazine in the trash can. A couple of minutes in, she suggested I go ahead and leave. I hugged them both. Sadness overwhelmed me. I loved them both, and her commitment to raising her grandson inspired me. Yet, it seemed harder than it should be. Disorientation swept over me. It felt like exile.

About a year later, one of those young men, now a legal adult, found himself in jail for a petty crime. He thought he might get a few months, or he might just get probation. It would take weeks, maybe even longer, to sort out. A few weeks earlier, he and his girlfriend had discovered that a new baby was on the way, and understandably he feared missing the birth. I'll never forget his phone calls from jail. Pain and regret dominated his emotions. "I just can't do this," he said over and over. I kept telling him we loved him. I kept telling him we wouldn't abandon him. I kept telling him God loved him. I kept telling him this did not define him. After hanging up from his phone calls, I'd just sit in silence. It shouldn't be this way. It shouldn't be so hard. It felt like exile.

Let me be clear. I loved every minute I spent with those teens and their families. Sharing life with them remains one of the greatest gifts I have ever received. We experienced far more good times than bad times. I could fill up page after page with all the funny stories. Yet, the hard times were really hard. Life is not as it should be. We live in exile, even as we've been called into a kingdom. We are a kingdom of exiles, experiencing a bit of heaven and a bit of hell every day.

Why is church so broken? Because we live in a broken world. Because we're broken people. But never forget this. We were created for something more. To be a kingdom of exiles means we live in hope and pursue our future despite our broken present. My first church, this stubborn resolute group of people, taught me this. Through all the challenges and imperfections, they continued to meet. Every Sunday, they broke bread and drank from the cup. They loved each other the best they knew how. We experienced and witnessed some intense tragedies in our time there. Yet on Sunday, they always sang. How can we sing the songs of Zion in a foreign land? We lean into the vision of the kingdom even as life feels like exile. As Paul says in 2 Corinthians 5:7, "We live by faith, not be sight." It's an act of defiance against the gloom of this world. This church taught me resilience, and for that I'll always be grateful.

Singing songs in a foreign land reminds me of *The Sound of Music*, the story of an Austrian singing family who fled rather than work for the Germans in World War II. As a kid, I remember the captivation I felt from watching Julie Andrews, Christopher Plummer, and all the children playing the Von Trapp family. Every time I've watched it, one scene always moves me the most. At the end, as they plan their escape from the Nazis, they find themselves at a singing competition. After the family performs, Captain von Trapp addresses the Austrian crowd. "I shall not be seeing you again perhaps for a very long time. I would sing for you now a love song. I know you share this love. I pray that you will never let it die." Then he begins to sing "Edelweiss," a patriotic ode to the Austrian homeland named for an indigenous flower. While singing, the Captain becomes overwhelmed with emotion, knowing everything has changed. He'll either live afar in exile or be captured and thrown in prison. It's as if he's thinking of Psalm 137. "How can I sing songs of Austria when the Nazis have taken over?" As he chokes up with emotion, his family joins him to keep the song going. He motions to the crowd, who joins in the singing. In doing so, they cope with exile. It's an act of defiance. By passing the song on to the next generation, they reach out to a future after the exile has ended. And be sure: it will end.

Years later, on another Good Friday, I got a difficult phone call. I heard news of more brokenness which would bring pain and heartache to the congregation I served. Why is church so hard? In the coming days, more and more people would find out, but on Easter Sunday hardly anyone knew. On that Sunday, Easter Sunday, I had been asked to offer the message. People have certain expectations for an Easter sermon—joy, optimism, and cheer. I felt none of those things. How can I sing of Zion in a foreign land? But then I remembered the promise of the gospel. Christ has come. Christ has risen. Christ will come again. If the gospel is true, then the exile will not last forever. The kingdom in its complete and full experience will come. So, with a spirit of resilience, I went to worship that Sunday. I preached the gospel, and I sang songs of Zion. It was an act of defiance against the reality of exile. Like the women who went to the tomb so long ago, I went in search of the body. But I didn't find a dead body. Instead, I found something beautiful.

9

The Body and the Bride

MY FRIENDS BOB AND Paul go way back. They grew up together in the same church in Alabama. Over the years, life events brought them each to Tennessee, and now their families participate in the same church, alongside my family. When I first met them, I marveled at the depth of their friendship, and then I found out why. Bob has one of Paul's kidneys. Years prior, when Bob needed a transplant, several volunteered. It turned out Paul's kidney was the best match. So Paul shared one with his lifelong friend. Now, Bob lives with part of Paul's body. They were already close, but this made them even closer. They share a connection that goes far beyond similar interests. They're bound together. On Sundays, as a church, we take Communion. We proclaim that because we eat Christ's body we have all become one body. For these guys, it's more than a metaphor.

Despite our mixed feelings about the church, Jesus clearly seems pretty crazy about her. Jesus loves the church. So as we process our relationship to her, it's wise to process how Jesus sees her. The Bible offers two main metaphors for how Jesus views the church, and together they usher us into a powerful reality. The church is both the body and bride of Jesus, and as we embrace this together we become family, with Jesus and each other.

Notice what the church is not. The church is not a building. We talk like that at times, but it's not true. It's both poor word usage and bad theology. The biblical word for church means assembly or gathering. But the church is not just any group that gathers for any reason. The church gathers to proclaim and connect with Jesus. Early Christians believed something deep, even mysterious occurred in the gathering. As they gathered to eat the body, they actually became the body. The church is the body of Christ, as Paul reminds us in 1 Corinthians 12:27. It's an organic illustration referencing a living people, not a lifeless building. The church represents a group of humans grafted into the divine essence of Jesus. Take this in, slowly. It's an incredibly optimistic view of what humans can become when gathered around Christ, and this power extends even as the gathered scatter out during the week.

Perhaps the most significant illustration of this in Scripture often gets missed. In the book of Acts, we find a zealous persecutor of the early church named Saul. Later, he'll become the famous apostle Paul. In Acts 9, he travels from Jerusalem north to Damascus with the intent of arresting Christians, but Jesus confronts him in verses 3-5.

> As he neared Damascus on his journey, suddenly a light from heaven flashed around him. He fell to the ground and heard a voice say to him, "Saul, Saul, why do you persecute me?" "Who are you, Lord?" Saul asked. "I am Jesus, whom you are persecuting," he replied.

For years, when I read this, I missed the connection Jesus made with the church. When Saul asks the identity of the voice, Jesus answers with "I am Jesus, whom you are persecuting." Saul persecuted the church, but Jesus says Saul persecuted him. At least according to Jesus, when you mess with the church, you mess with him. In college, I hung out a lot with some friends who were twin sisters. We used to joke with them. "Do you feel each other's pain? If one of you falls down, does the other feel it?" As you can imagine, they got tired of this line of questioning. I assume all twins get tired of these jokes. But with Jesus, it's real. If you hurt the church, Jesus feels it. Why? They are the same body.

The metaphor shows the hopeful expectations Jesus holds for the church. At the Last Supper, Jesus invites the apostles to eat and drink the bread and cup, telling them it is his body and blood. Then, after the supper, in John 14:12, he tells them, "Very truly I tell you, whoever believes in me will do the works I have been doing, and they will do even greater things than these, because I am going to the Father." Jesus expects his followers to continue his movement when he leaves. We should be doing the same things Jesus did in his ministry. We must pursue reconciliation, seek justice, eat with the outcasts, feed the hungry, heal the sick, and love our neighbors, even our enemies.

Section 2: Beautiful

The church lives as the presence of Christ in the world, the continuation of the Jesus movement. We use the word "incarnation" to describe Jesus' time on earth. Jesus showed up as God in the flesh. In similar fashion, the church lives as an incarnation, Jesus in the flesh. The resurrected body of Jesus ascended to heaven, yet Christ still has a body on the planet, the church. Jesus lives and works on earth through the church.

That's the goal, at least. How have we done? In John 14:7, Jesus says, "If you really know me, you will know my Father." Apply that one step further. If we become the body of Christ, the continuation of the Jesus movement fueled by the Spirit, then we should also be able to say this. "If you really know the church, then you know Jesus." For some, this resonates. It has been your experience. For others, this proves frustrating. Some might laugh or even cry. They knew the church but saw no sign of Jesus. It's an inspiring but intimidating calling. It's hard to live up to that hype.

Some months ago, I took my girls to see *Frozen 2*. They loved *Frozen* and eagerly anticipated seeing the sequel. As we sat there waiting for the credits to end, I wondered if any movie could live up to that hype. It got me thinking about sequels. While *Frozen 2* fared well in my view, I rarely enjoy sequels. I find they rarely live up to the original. I think of a film from my teen years. In 1994, I walked into a theater with friends to see *Speed*, knowing nothing. You may remember that film, starring Keanu Reeves, Sandra Bullock, and Dennis Hopper. The plot centers on a bus that can never dip below 55 miles per hour due to a bomb on board. Filmed on a 33-million-dollar budget, it made over 350 million, a true sleeper hit. Just three years later, I eagerly went to see the sequel, *Speed 2*. Not all of the same actors came back. The plot lacked originality. It paled in comparison to the first one.

In contrast, many regard *The Godfather Part II* as the greatest sequel of all time. After all, it's the only sequel to win the Academy Award for Best Picture. The film succeeds in what all sequels desire. It takes all the characters, themes, and plot of the original and extends them to their logical conclusion, with a few surprises thrown in. For those who want to know what happens next in the life of Michael Corleone, played by Al Pacino, the sequel shows them. For those who want to know more about what made the Corleone family, the sequel shows them with classic flashback scenes starring Robert De Niro. It's a near-perfect sequel.

Jesus envisions this for the church. If Jesus' life on earth comes as the original, then the life of the church rises as the sequel. How does the church measure up, though? Is the church *Speed 2* or *Godfather Part II*? Probably both, at times. I've seen some bad Jesus sequels, and yet, I've seen some that were spot on. Those keep me coming back.

I think of a dear mentor who passed away last year. I came to know Buford Eubanks in the last decade of his life, as we worshipped together in the same church. A retired vice president in a well-known company in our town, Buford exuded humility and kindness. When I ran into employees from his former company, they always smiled at the mention of his name. He worked in human resources, and many spoke of his conscientious care of employees and advocacy for worker's benefits. He served as an elder in our church, yet he never lorded his authority over others. He always seemed to be cleaning—sweeping, mopping, and taking out the trash. Frequently, people walked in from the streets asking for help—food, a bus pass, or a hotel room for the night. They always asked, "Is Buford around?" They all knew him. They all had a story of a time he helped them. Buford was even known to let unhoused people live in the church building from time to time. One of these men was a man named Charlie. These two men couldn't be more different, at least in the ways the world measures difference. Yet, I often found them talking together. In fact, Charlie frequently came looking for Buford, not anyone else in our church. About a month after Buford died, Charlie stopped by the church. He hadn't yet heard of Buford's passing. When I told him, he began to weep. Through the tears, he told us things we'd never heard about Buford, previously untold acts of generosity and hospitality.

In many ways, from a religious perspective, Buford was what you might call old school. At times, he used church jargon from the 1950s. Buford liked to sing old hymns and loved the New King James Version of the Bible. Yet, he led a church full of adults half his age. When I first arrived, I wondered about this. Why did a younger group of Christians who were not what you might call old school follow the leadership of Buford? They saw something in him. Put better, they saw someone in him. While imperfect, Buford loved his neighbors. He took time for strangers. He stopped to talk to children and knew their names. He led by grabbing a broom. He sacrificed for his family and church. I never heard him say a mean thing about anyone or anything. In short, Buford was a good sequel of Jesus.

Still, there's a lot of bad sequels out there. I'm not the Christian I need to be, and if you met Buford, he'd tell you he wasn't either. How can Jesus still love us when we act like this? How can Christ still forgive us when we sully his legacy as we do? Because we are his bride. This metaphor surfaces in Jesus' parables, Paul's words in Ephesians 5, and John's vision from Revelation. What wisdom does it offer us?

Growing up, I didn't care much for weddings. I didn't like to dress up. Romance didn't make sense to me. I didn't get what it was all about. But then, like many of you, I fell in love. I remember the first time I saw Beth. A few months back, while visiting the college campus where we met, I walked through the parking lot where that first meeting happened years ago. Emotion and gratitude overwhelmed me. Every now and then, I drive by the church building where we married. I'll never forget how she looked when she walked down the aisle. It's a moment I'll never forget. Now, I like going to weddings, because I love that moment. I love to watch how the bride and groom look at each other. You can see the anticipation, the intense longing, the complete joy, and the total admiration.

Jesus is smitten with the church. He loves the church, his bride. Her weaknesses do not scare him away. Her sins do not make him reconsider his vows. Some say the church has lost her way. Some can't get past her brokenness. I agree in many ways. Yet, I contend that Jesus is still in love with her. Deep down, I wonder at times how God can love us, how he can love me. Then I consider the extent to which Jesus pursued us. I consider the overwhelming grace and excessive forgiveness of Jesus. Jesus is crazy about the church. He's crazy about you.

Perhaps, the most intense evidence of this metaphor comes from the story of Hosea. God called him to a type of performance art to illustrate a truth to himself and others. God told Hosea to marry an unfaithful woman. That seems like such a bizarre thing to us. Why would God call him to that? God wanted Hosea to understand God's role as a loyal spouse in the midst of betrayal. Only through this experience will Hosea truly know how God's love exceeds the brokenness of the unfaithful spouse. Only through this marriage will Hosea understand the grace exercised in the marriage of Yahweh and Israel, Christ and the church.

The church has cheated on Jesus. We thought he wasn't looking, and we committed adultery with the gods of this world. We violated our vows. I wouldn't blame him if he left, but he didn't leave. More than stay, he loves us more than ever. He forgave us. Jesus kept on loving us. Christ refuses to turn on his bride. His love is that good, that strong.

This overwhelmingly good news brings us to a life-altering realization. The body metaphor shows us our calling to continue his movement while the bride metaphor shows his unconditional love for us when we fail. Together, the metaphors of the body and the bride take us to this truth. We're part of Jesus. We're married. The church is a family.

At the church of my youth, I commonly heard people referred to as "brother so-and-so" or "sister so-and-so." For some, it probably just served as church talk, but for many, it was real. They actually treated each other like family. They sacrificed for each other. Plenty did for me. At some point, this type of language got rare, at least in the circles I run in. However, my church has the blessing of a sister church in our neighborhood. We regularly join together with this congregation, which talks like this. Friends like William and Tyrone walk up to me and call me brother, and they act like they mean it. Language like this creates a welcoming atmosphere as well as calling us to live up to it. When I hear that brother and sister talk, it reminds me of the church of my youth. It reminds me of the spiritual family that raised me. It may seem over the top to some, but when you're the one in need of a family, it means something.

For many, church is the closest thing to family that they have. I think back to my friends Paul and Bob. When I first met them, it was a devastating time. Bob and his wife, Ashley, had a son named Ian, who only lived five months, never leaving the hospital because of a heart condition. When I joined their church, Ian was three months old. I watched this church take care of each other like family. I watched as they prayed and visited Bob, Ashley, and Ian. I saw the heartache they all experienced over his condition. As his final hours neared, they kept loving each other. I remember Ian's funeral. The church was there. Afterwards, we all had a big meal together. We cried and shared stories. We talked about Ian's beautiful, piercing eyes. As I looked around at the church, they acted like they'd lost a family member. In a way they had. They were family, sharing the same body, even the same name. When Bob and Ashley named their son, they thought of his father's kidney. Ian Paul Hoskins was family.

A few years later, our congregation discussed a controversial topic. By this time, Ashley and Bob had another child, a daughter. She has Ian's eyes. On this particular day, it was my turn to address the topic in our Sunday conversation. I'd prepared comments that aligned with my convictions. Some would agree with me, and some would not be. Within my prepared remarks, I had a few zingers I hoped to throw in to achieve the desired result. Like anyone, I wanted to get my way on the issue. Before I began, Ashley walked up and put a finger in my face. "Hey, don't mess this up.

Don't split this church. For some of us, this is the only family we've got."
I'm a couple of years older than her, and yet I just said, "Yes ma'am." I took
out the zingers. I stuck to my convictions, but as I taught, I traded pride for
humility and winning for dialogue. I did what she asked. I didn't split the
church, the only family she had.

10

The Washing and the Table

ON JANUARY 28, 1986, I woke up to snow on the ground. School was cancelled. I still remember the elation I felt. As a child of two schoolteachers, these days got as close to perfection as possible. None of us had to go anywhere. We could sled, build snowmen, and drink hot chocolate without interruption. However, on this day, something even more exciting lay on the schedule. The Challenger space shuttle would be launched, and since we'd all be home, we could watch it together on television.

We'd been looking forward to the Challenger launch for quite some time because of Christa McAuliffe. The previous year, she'd been selected from over eleven thousand applicants as part of the NASA Teacher in Space Project. She would be the first teacher in space, and we looked forward to the lessons she would teach during the mission. Since both my parents were school teachers, this hit close to home. Even more unique, my mother was the same age as Christa McAuliffe, with the exact hairstyle. I remember thinking how similar they looked. I imagined what it would feel like if my mother prepared to go into space.

As you know, shortly into launch, the Challenger exploded, and all seven crewmembers died. For the first time in my life, I saw someone die in real time. We just sat there for a second, confused over what had happened. I remember hearing the commentators scramble for answers. At that age, I don't recall any firm conclusions or thought processes. I just felt sad. I can't remember if I knew then or later in the day that she was dead. Christa McAuliffe, a schoolteacher similar to my mother in looks and age, died.

What started off as a great day became one of the most disillusioning days of my childhood.

While I'm sure I couldn't express it at the time, I remember feeling a profound sense of "It shouldn't be this way." I experienced a sizable sense of loss, both for those who had died as well as for my sense of innocence. I got that far-from-home feeling, the exile feeling I spoke about earlier. In the creation story, we find Eden to be a place of goodness and order. We discover Eden to be a place of abundant beauty and love, a place of God's presence. Whatever this experience was, it was not Eden. Like Adam and Eve, I felt on the outside of Eden and didn't know how to get back.

My mother died later the same year. That day, August 30, 1986, became the most disillusioning day of my life. The type of tragedy that had been on screen became personal. Grief and loss came near, not as abstract categories out there but as an up-close and personal reality. With considerably more intensity than back in January, I felt far from home. My life was not supposed to go down like this. I was outside of Eden once again. Every year on January 28, a news feed will reference the anniversary of the Challenger explosion. Every year when this happens, I think of my mother.

Like many people, one of my responses to grief, past or present, lies in the search for and embrace of nostalgia. That wistful, sentimental desire to return to the past brings me hope. Memories from the past remind me that joy is possible. You might call them memories of Eden. One such memory comes from that same fateful year.

In July of 1986, my parents, maternal grandparents, brother, and I went on a month-long trip to the American Northeast. We drove up the east coast in our RV through the Middle Atlantic and New England states. We ventured up into Quebec and Montreal, saw Niagara Falls, and then gradually made our way back home. Perhaps my favorite memory of the trip came on our visit to Bar Harbor, Maine and nearby Acadia National Park. After a day of searching out lighthouses, beaches, and rocky coastlines, we took a walk through the town at dusk. I have this picture seared in my brain. We walked through a town park eating ice cream. I remember a gazebo. I remember lights. It was a perfect summer night. Granny and Gramps were there. Mom and Dad, as well as my brother, were there. Everything was perfect. This was Eden. Over the years, I pulled out this memory when I felt homesick, homesick for Eden. Over time, I forgot it happened in Bar Harbor. I just knew it happened somewhere in the Northeast.

Years later, in April of 2002, Beth and I had been married for just a few months and were living in New England. We had a Friday-Saturday with no plans, so we drove the six hours up the coastline to Bar Harbor. After a little hiking and biking, we took a walk through the town. Suddenly, out of nowhere, I saw the gazebo. It all came back. I was there again like I had been before. I felt transported. In a way I can't fully explain, I felt my mother's presence. Her memory came alive. The beauty of that moment came back to me. It was a memory, but it was more than a memory. It felt like we were together again, as if the past had met the future. The intensity of the moment knocked me over. I literally had to sit down. I felt a mix of sadness and joy, a powerful dose of nostalgia. The beautiful reality of it all surrounded me.

I've long marveled at the close but complicated relationship between the past and the future. We struggle with the past. We want to recapture it, to erase it, or even to change it. We want to control it. It haunts us. It motivates us. At times, it shows up again. When it comes to the bad stuff, we want to understand, to fix, and prevent. When it comes to the good stuff, we want to hold on, relive, and secure. Our understanding of the past shapes the future we desire. Our past experiences shape the person we want to become in the future.

For me, seemingly innocuous things like January 28 on the calendar and a gazebo in Bar Harbor serve as interpretive markers. They hold deep meaning for how I understand the past and pursue the future. In a sense, they serve as portals linking what has been to what could be. They tie who I've been to who I want to be. As humans, we gravitate to these interpretive paradigms, these ways of understanding ourselves and our world.

God made us like this, so it's no accident that God provided the church with central practices that enable us to interpret the past and future. Many Christians call these sacraments. They exist as vessels of the sacred which form a connection between heaven and earth, between the past and future. They remind us of how God embraces our brokenness and makes us beautiful. These mysterious practices mediate a connection, an experience. Our purpose is not to completely understand them but to submit to the reality they proclaim. Throughout church history, baptism and Communion have been the premier and most consistent sacraments. Through them, we understand and encounter the risen Christ. Through them, we deal with our past and become empowered to live into a redeemed future for the good of others.

While this may seem obvious, it should be stated. Christians believe Jesus to be the most important figure in human history. Christians believe the thirty years Jesus walked on the earth, especially his ministry and even more so his passion week, to be the most significant time period in history. But Christians do not just see these as past events. Through the sacraments, Christians connect these past events to the present. As Paul explains in Romans 6, we experience the death, burial, and resurrection of Christ in baptism. When we experience baptism, we connect to Jesus. We experience Christ. Our baptism is a portal linking us to not only his baptism but the cross and empty tomb. In addition, Jesus explained his death and resurrection through the lens of the Passover lamb. He embraced and fulfilled the meaning of the Passover supper by making it his supper, the Lord's Supper. He called the bread his body and the cup his blood. Much more than a ritual, when we sit at the table, we not only ingest Christ, but we meet Christ. When we break bread at the table, we're transported to his Passover table long ago. These sacraments connect the past to our present in order to prepare us for the future. In this, Jesus is indeed "the Alpha and the Omega, the first and the last, the beginning and end" of all things (Rev 22:13).

In this manner, the practices of baptism and Communion serve as an interpretive map. They offer a tangible way to make meaning and find our location in this world. I think back to the apex of malls in the 1980s and 1990s. I remember the hustle and bustle of Christmas time at the mall. I remember getting lost and stumbling upon the big mall maps. Every time, I'd look for the star which was labeled, "You Are Here." From there, I could see where I'd been and where I wanted to go. This gave me a reorientation that delivered me from my disorientation. This is what the sacraments do. You are here, and you want to go there. This is how you get there. I'm convinced that our most basic life questions find resolution in Jesus. Who are we? Why are we here? Where are we going? I'm convinced that we'll find illumination when we meet Jesus in baptism and Communion. The washing and the table form the foundation of church practice, our common life together.

As a child, nothing seemed as mysterious to me as baptism. We heard that one dip in the water would take away every bad thing you'd ever done. We heard that if you went under the water, you'd come out full of the Holy Spirit. Sometimes, people said "Holy Ghost," which added to the mystery. At the church of my youth, the baptistry lay beyond easy access. Playing after church, we'd go back behind the Communion table and jump up to try to see it. At times, we'd even try to scale the wall and climb, just for the chance of getting to stick our hand in the seemingly magic water. Our baptistry had a water heater on a timer. Therefore, around worship times, the water felt like bath water. The warm inviting feel of the water added yet another layer to the sense of mystery. On each side of the front of the auditorium, there were doors that led to changing rooms for males and females to prepare for baptism. On a few occasions, we snuck inside those rooms, which led to steps down to the baptistry. We'd dip our toe in the water. It felt so wondrous.

It wasn't the only time I saw someone dip their toe in the water and be filled with wonder. Gramps, my maternal grandfather, often did this on trips. We'd go up to some river or lake or ocean or mountain stream, and he'd go immediately to the edge. He'd sit and take his shoe off. He'd dip his toe in the water. One such example stood out for its sheer absurdity. One summer, two years after my mother passed, the five of us (Granny, Gramps, Dad, and my older brother) went to Alaska. Granny and Gramps had always wanted to go, and they didn't want to go alone. We did several of the normal Alaskan adventures, including an Alaskan cruise and a train ride near Mt. Denali. One day was a little different, though. From Fairbanks, near the middle of the state, we took a small plane up to Point Barrow, the northernmost city in the United States. From there a bus took us to the edge of the Arctic Ocean. We wore heavy coats as we slowly walked to the edge of the Arctic. Thick ice loomed everywhere, but at the edge someone had broken a small patch of ice. You could see the water. Gramps went straight for it. He sat right down there, and in the bitter cold he took his shoe and sock off one foot. He put his toe in the water with an intense look of joy on his face. Sensing that I found this curious, he smiled at me and said, "It's for your mother. It's what she would do." In this moment, based on the look on his face, he felt closer to her. The agony of her loss eased a bit. I know it did for me.

The lure of the water finally drew me in. The mystery of the washing became too much to resist. The next summer, May 30, 1989, to be exact, Gramps baptized me on a Wednesday night. Honestly, no bolt of lightning or road-to-Damascus experience moved me to it. I'd always wanted to do it. Middle school lay on the fall horizon. Surely, another summer of church camp would compel other kids and teens to do it. I might as well get on the front of that wave and hop in. It was time. My life had been ebbing towards this moment, and I felt no resistance.

I'd lived enough life to know I wasn't the person I needed to be. Looking back, my greatest sins probably revolved around teasing other kids at times and not promptly obeying my father and other adults in authority. I knew I hadn't committed murder or robbed a bank, and yet, I'd been taught all sins were the same. I'd sinned, and I needed forgiveness. I was broken, and I needed to be washed.

I'll never forget that night. I remember my nervousness. I remember the feel of the water. I remember the grip of my grandfather. I remember the silence when I went under water. I remember the elation when I came up. It did not disappoint. It felt just as mysterious as I'd hoped. My sins were gone. The Holy Spirit was inside of me. I'd done what my parents had done. I'd done what Christians had done for two thousand years. I'd done what Jesus had done. I felt connected to all of them. Something, someone that seemed far off had come near. Jesus was present. It was all so beautiful.

Over the years, I've witnessed countless baptisms and baptized some myself. I've seen friends baptized in rivers, lakes, swimming pools, and cattle troughs. I've seen people lining up for baptism at revivals. I've baptized a friend in a vacant sanctuary with only one witness. Every single one has moved me. The mystery holds up. Most every time, it seems so simple, too simple. At times, I wonder why we make all the fuss. But then I'm reminded why. I see the anticipation. I see the community. I see the change in their life. I feel the presence of Christ.

Admittedly, I've seen my fair share of baptized believers who seemingly demonstrated no life change. But far more often, I've seen change. As Paul says in Galatians 2:20, "I am crucified with Christ, and I no longer. Yet not I but Christ, lives in me. And the life I live in the flesh, I live by faith in the Son of God who loved me and gave himself for me." Over and over, I've seen people change, mature, and become more like Christ after being baptized. It's happened too many times for me not to believe in it.

Every time we practice baptism, we take brokenness seriously. We take sin, repentance, and confession seriously. We refuse to cover up our wrongs. We own it. At the same time, we proclaim forgiveness. We claim grace. We embrace change. We believe no one is beyond redemption. Every person, no matter what they've done, can have a different ending, a beautiful ending to their story.

Gramps believed this. For twenty-five years, he went to the Nashville City Jail most every single Sunday. He helped lead a worship service. Eventually, it grew to two worship services. Gramps and others proclaimed the gospel to the male inmates. Granny did her part to encourage the female inmates. They told them God would forgive them no matter what they'd done. They told them change was possible. They sought to empathize with them for the injustice of this world. When I turned eighteen, Gramps handed me the paperwork to go with him some. I don't remember him asking me. He just assumed I'd want to go. They had this little portable baptistry contraption right there in the jail. Over the decades, Gramps baptized one thousand inmates in the jail. Perhaps some just did that to feel less guilty. Perhaps some never lived changed lives. Of course, we need to offer more than just baptism to those who want a different life, freedom from their past as well as the injustice around them. I can think of at least ten reasons to be cynical, yet I can think of far more to be hopeful. When we proclaim baptism, we proclaim forgiveness, change, and hope. We proclaim Jesus, and he is with us.

Every Sunday in jail, Gramps served them the Lord's Supper. Communion, like baptism, ushers us into the mysterious presence of Jesus. When we pass the trays at my church on Sundays, one of my girls will often sit in my lap. As I grab the bread, I will whisper in her ear, "This is the body of Christ, broken for you." Inevitably, on more than one occasion, she will giggle. "It's a cracker, Dad. It's not Jesus' body." I smile and say, "Oh, but it is Jesus' body. It represents his body, and he's with us right now." She giggles with glee. She begs me for a bite. Even though our tradition normally believes that only the baptized should take Communion (and we practice believer's baptism), I often give in and give her a tiny taste. I can't refuse her. Everyone loves a mystery.

Since my baptism thirty years ago, I've probably taken Communion over 1,500 times with over 300,000 people. I've taken Communion in Canada, Mexico, Honduras, the United Kingdom, and Italy. I've taken Communion with rich and poor, liberals and conservatives, rural and urban residents. For centuries, theologians have offered theories of what happens at Communion complete with fancy, impressive words like transubstantiation and consubstantiation. While I can't fully explain what happens at the table, I can say this: The consistent practice of being at the table with others changes you.

At the Lord's Table, we encounter both a vertical and horizontal dimension. The table connects us to the head, Christ, as well as other humans seated alongside us. The table follows the path of the First and Second Commandments, to love God and neighbor. When we dine at the table, God meets us there. Over the last year, to prepare for teaching a study-abroad college course in Italy, I studied the life of Leonardo da Vinci. Specifically, stories revolving around his painting of the Last Supper moved me. While most famous paintings in Europe were meant for royalty or an impressive church sanctuary, Leonardo painted this famous work on the wall of a dining hall. Moreover, he painted the angles and windows of the work to fit in with the room. If seated in the dining hall, the Last Supper looks like an extension of the actual room. It looks real and present. You don't feel like you're just looking at a painting. You feel like you're part of the Last Supper. Leonardo was onto something, for I believe God intends every Lord's Supper to feel this way. We're not just reenacting an ancient tradition. We're eating with Christ. We're eating Christ. He's feeding us. We're spending time with him. We're not alone. Christ is with us.

I remember my mother's favorite table. In fact, most every night I eat at the same table. A couple of years before she died, my mother saved up and bought the table of her dreams. She and my dad bought a dining room set made of cherrywood. I can picture the day it came home because I built a huge fort with all the boxes. For months, I kept the biggest box as my clubhouse. It was not our everyday table but sat in the dining room for special occasions. When my dad married my second mom and our family doubled in size, we had to use it all the time. The four of us messy kids put a beating on that table. So, my second mom gave it to her mother, and we bought another, more pragmatic table. Still, as the years went by, I got to eat at my first mother's table every time I visited my step-grandmother. Eventually, as she moved into assisted living, she gave the table to me. The cherry dining room table came to my house. Oddly enough, my wife and I had just bought a dining room table that fit our house. Honestly, my mother's table was way too nice for my three little kids to eat on every day. I didn't want to mess it up. However, we decided that using it makes more sense than putting it in storage. So, every few days, I put a clean tablecloth on my mother's cherry table. Daily we gather around her table. I confess I don't think of her every day, but on the days I change the tablecloth, when I see the nicks and bruises we've put on the table, I think of her. What would she think of my life? Am I living in a way that honors her? This is what you do when you sit around someone's table. Surely, we do this around the Lord's Table. What does Jesus think of my life? Am I living in a way that honors him?

This leads us to the horizontal perspective of the table. As we first consider our relationship with God, we then look at those beside us. To be right with God implies we seek to be right with each other. To love God means we should love each other. This is no private, individualist religious observance. It's a social act. Jesus shows us this in the John 13 story of the Last Supper. He humbles himself by washing everyone's feet. Immediately uncomfortable with this, the disciples try to stop him. Yet, he completes the act as an example and tells them to go out and do likewise. As we sit at the table with each other, we assess our obedience to the command to love one another. When we gather around the table, we ask, "Does everyone have a place at the table?" As we eat at the table, we ask, "Does everyone have food?" As we drink at the table, we ask, "Is anyone thirsty?"

If you're able to dine at the Lord's Table and not consider the social implications of the meal, you're missing out. I say this as a statement of confession, for I know I've too often practiced cognitive dissonance around the sacrament. The Lord's Table shapes all tables. The meal shapes all meals. It forces us to ask who is left out. Who is neglected, abandoned, and marginalized? Who is hungry and thirsty? Why? What are we called to do? What does "washing feet" look like for us today?

The table provides a framework to address our most daunting social problems of today. How do we address poverty? Consider the table. How do we heal loneliness? Meet around the table. How do we repent of and make right the racism and sexism around us and in us? Go to the table. We can't just go through the motions and move on. We have to meet with Christ and let him shape us.

In 1 Corinthians 11, Paul talks about a group who went through the motions of the table but didn't really dine with the Lord. They didn't let the meal shape all meals. They didn't dine in a way that encompassed the First and Second Commandments. They didn't share. They fostered a culture of haves and have-nots. Paul scolded them by telling them it wasn't really the Lord's Supper if they acted that way. We must be intentional about our practices. Taking Communion in the right way involves more than frequency, content (grape juice or wine), or who serves it. Taking Communion in the right way means we eat with Jesus, and we let him change us. As Jesus changes us, he'll change the world.

The sacraments of baptism and Communion exist as interpretive signposts, bridges if you will, connecting the past and future. When it comes to the past, our society gives us numerous unwise postures. Some refuse to consider the past. Some simply erase it. Some act like it's all that matters. Some act like it doesn't matter at all. We hold similar unwise postures towards the future. Some believe it's inevitable. Some believe it all depends on our own effort.

In contrast, baptism says we have to confront our broken past, but it does not define us. We move beyond our past by facing it and connecting it with death, the death of Christ. Once we die, we experience new life. We gain a new Spirit, which holds the potential for a new way of living. As we meet at the table, we consider all the unjust and unequal tables of this world. We confront our complicity in that. Yet, Christ forgives us yet again and feeds us. He continually adds chairs to the table and sends us out to make all tables like his table. With a healed and forgiven past and the power to be different in the future, we enter a beautiful present in the presence of Jesus.

Throughout my life, the two practices of baptism and Communion have changed me. I experience Jesus through them, and I remember what I must do. When I encounter temptation, I think of him. When I pursue reconciliation, I remember him. When I spend time with the poor, he comes to my mind. When I see a friend or stranger in doubt or filled with fear, Jesus is there. Jesus meets me in these times. Jesus is alive. I see him in the washing and the table. I remember that while we are broken, Jesus has made us beautiful.

A few years ago, my dad took me and my three brothers to Glacier National Park. For three straight days, we took incredible hikes. One particular all-day hike took us to Iceberg Lake. As we came over the final hill, we looked down at this postcard lake with mountain peaks surrounding it. A few huge chunks of ice lay in the water. I knew exactly what I had to do. I walked straight to the water's edge. I took off my shoes and socks. I put my toe in the water. It's what Gramps would do. It's what Mom would do. So I did it, in remembrance of them.

11

Open Weekly Gatherings

IN THE FIRST FEW years after my mother's death, I often felt a deep void. During the day, I distracted myself with school, friends, cartoons, and Nintendo. But late at night, as I tried to fall asleep, it came—the deep sense of isolation. I missed my mother's touch, and I felt the absence of her presence. I lay there at night missing her and wondering if the feeling would last forever.

At this time in my life, I shared a bed with my older brother. He's always been a source of strength and support, but like many brotherly relationships, we didn't always get along. We both played together and fought together at times. We always loved each other, but it wasn't always touchy feely if you know what I mean. We didn't hug as my daughters do now. We valued our personal space. But on these nights, when I couldn't sleep, I would reach out my leg and place it on his leg. My ankle lay on top of his ankle. In a way I couldn't explain and still don't understand, that simple touch assuaged my loneliness and took away a bit of my isolation. My prickly older brother never said a word. He never mentioned it, but I'm sure he knew what was going on. As one of the wiser people I've known, he knew.

Sharing that story now, I wonder what I would have done without that. What if I'd not had a brother to put my leg on? What if a physical connection had not been available? More than just the availability of my brother's presence, the steady frequency of his presence proved enormous. It sounds funny to say, but his leg was always there for me.

In American culture today, we live busy, scattered lives. Availability and accessibility prove rare. Many commute long distances. We overschedule and overcommit. We surround ourselves with the noise of TV, radio, podcasts, and social media. We wish we had more time for the things we truly love. We have friends we want to see more, but, overwhelmed by work and family commitments, many struggle to schedule community.

In our culture, we have a hard time putting community on the calendar. I think of my college buddies. We've scattered across various states—Maryland, Tennessee, and Texas. We all have children and responsibilities. We work hard to see each other every two to three years. Just doing that takes a Herculean act of scheduling strength. Yet, that's not how we became so close. We became close friends through frequent, accessible contact. We grew close through availability and accessibility. Long before kids and marriage, we hung out in each other's dorm rooms every day late into the night. For relationships to form, strengthen, and continue, we need a schedule.

From the earliest of times, the church has offered this, a schedule for finding community. We might take it for granted. We might not even realize the uniqueness of it at first. As we compare the church to other social relationships, a clear strength arises quickly. Churches offer a weekly opportunity to make, keep, and spend time with friends. Churches offer frequent, accessible contact. One of the core beauties of the church lies in its open, weekly gatherings.

Gramps was a storyteller. Like many storytellers, he had a few favorites that he liked to repeat. He liked to tell about his wedding day while he served as a navigation instructor on leave from an Air Force base in Texas. My grandparents got married in middle Tennessee, and as they moved west, he liked to point out that Granny had never been west of the Tennessee River. When he got tired, he let her drive, despite the fact that she'd never driven before. When she asked how to drive, he simply said, "Keep it between the ditches." He always laughed at that part, and she did too. Growing up in the decade after World War I, he often told stories of war heroes such as Eddie Rickenbacker and Alvin C. York. As he got older, he seemed to tell these stories more often. As he did this on one family occasion, I turned to my father. "Do you think he's losing his memory? He always tells the same stories." My dad smiled and said, "He's not losing his memory. He doesn't tell the story because he forgets. He tells the story so that you won't forget."

Let me share one story he never wanted me to forget. During the early 1940s, Gramps served as a navigation instructor near San Antonio. During this time, he heard that a local congregation in Hondo, Texas, forty miles west of San Antonio, had quit meeting together. In essence, this small church had folded. This news really saddened him, so he drove out to Hondo. He tracked down members of the congregation and started gathering them together again on Sundays. He organized the services and quickly got others involved. As he told the story, within weeks the church was up and running again.

Until his death, Gramps told this story. It always stood out to me because he seemed to have a much greater appreciation for congregations getting together than most people I know. As I became a teenager and studied history, it struck me even more. As the world engaged in a great war, Gramps focused on getting a tiny country church going again. As Hitler threatened to take over the world, Gramps spent his weekends meeting with a small group of disciples in a tiny town well off the world's stage. During the spring break of 1989, my fifth-grade year, we took a trip down to Texas with my grandparents. It served as a memorable introduction to Texas, the state where I'd later live. We went across the border to Laredo, Mexico. We visited the Alamo in San Antonio. Then, one day, we drove the forty miles out to Hondo, Texas. We drove up to a little, non-descript building with a church sign out front. We weren't there on a Sunday. The building was locked up, but presumably a group continued to meet there on Sundays. Right on cue, Gramps stood there and told us the story yet again. "I heard there was a church that had given up meeting. So, I drove out there on the weekends and got them meeting again."

As a social group, one of the most unique characteristics of a church is this: open, weekly gatherings. Churches offer frequent, accessible meetings. It's on the calendar. Fifty-two Sundays a year, all around the world, you can attend an open gathering of believers. Every week, people enter gatherings which they have never attended prior. Many attend because of an invitation from a friend. Still, many walk in not knowing anyone. Maybe they come because of a mysterious leading. Maybe they come for a particular type of support or assistance. Maybe they come to connect with God. Maybe they're just plain lonely.

Consider the story of Frank and Maggie. They moved to Tennessee from Ohio for their jobs. They didn't really know anyone. In many ways, they were starting over. One Sunday, they just walked into our open, weekly gathering. Slowly, I got to know them. We had them in our home for dinner. They became part of our community. They made deep friendships. Within a few months, they were delivering food to the sick and helping with our homeless ministry. They became an active, strong part of our community. After a year or so, I asked them how many friends they had in town. A few but not a ton. Most of their friends were from church. Consider why that is. On one hand, you could argue that spiritual community makes strong community, with which I agree. You could also say they made specific choices which led to this outcome, with which I agree as well. But, taking a step back, there's a simple additional reason why church relationships happened so easily. Churches offer weekly, open gatherings which are accessible and frequent. For someone looking for connection, it's an essential ingredient.

Often, I run into a friend while I'm out and about in town. We do the typical, "Hey, good to see you. We should get together sometime." Then a frustration sets in. It's so hard to schedule. Sometimes it's a month or so before we can even schedule a time to meet for coffee. I have amazing, lifelong friends that live in the same city whom I see once or twice a year. Modern life pursues a frenetic pace. It's hard to schedule community. Our pace makes our relationships distant and thin. We need a rhythm conducive to relationships.

For centuries, the church has offered this rhythm. From the earliest times, the church offered frequency and accessibility, as seen in the New Testament book of Acts. The Jesus movement never centered on private values in private lives. It never focused on isolated personal devotion. The Christian movement has always been about social connection empowered by God for the common good. Clearly, the church grew because of the power of God. However, we should not minimize an aspect clearly used by God—frequent accessibility.

Take a moment to consider the accessibility of churches. They meet in set locations at set times. Their meetings take on a consistency missing in other areas of life. The church I'm currently a part of has cancelled its Sunday service once in the last twenty years due to snow. Making that math explicit, out of the last 1,040 Sundays, they met on 1,039 of those days. Even during the COVID-19 pandemic, we continued to meet virtually. When you come to a church, you don't have to say anything. You don't have to pay anything. You don't have to believe anything. There's no litmus test to be there.

Yes, I know many have not been welcomed in churches, and that's sad and wrong. However, from the beginning, churches always maintained a low bar for entry. Yes, to join or become a leader, one has to profess and model certain beliefs. But to walk in the door and meet people, there's no hurdle to jump over. It's completely open.

I remember when the following story happened to my friend and mentor Richard. Years ago, he noticed a guest walk into Sunday service. Richard greeted him, learned his name was Jack, and helped him find a seat. Throughout the morning, Richard watched many others chat with Jack, but he didn't seem to have any previous relationships with anyone there. After the service, Jack didn't go anywhere. He just hung around in the foyer, sort of like he was waiting on something to happen. Noticing this, Richard went up and invited him to lunch with his family. Once they got to the appointed restaurant, Richard and Jack sat at one end of the table together. Richard simply asked, "What brings you our way this morning?" Jack said, "Well, I just got in from Georgia yesterday. I hit a rough patch and needed a fresh start. I pulled into a motel last night, and I hardly have any money. I don't know what to do. An older friend of mine told me to find a church and wait around until somebody invited me to lunch. Then, I should do whatever that person tells me. So, what do you think I should do?" Richard became his friend, mentor, and advocate. He helped him get a job and an apartment. They spent a significant amount of time together in the following weeks and months. Jack's life got better because of this friendship, this community. It all started with an accessible, open gathering. On Sunday Jack knew where to go, and people still do.

Some come to find friendship. Many of the people who walk in not knowing anyone come out of deep loneliness. This may be the most common reason I've observed. Think about it. If you move to a new town for a job, how do you make friends? Let's say you've left family and friends miles away to take this job. You might hang out with friends from work a bit. You might join a book club, yoga class, or softball team. Yet, all of those involve certain skills and interests and maybe even money. If you just want to meet and talk to people, where do you go? No group has as low a bar for entry as the church.

Some come for help raising their children. Raising kids might be among the hardest things we humans do. Many parents feel overwhelmed. They want an extra set of hands. They need other adults looking out for their kids. They desire the proverbial village to mold and guard their kids. Normally, they want some help on basic moral teaching. Often, they want some help on teaching their kids what life is really about and how to find purpose. Always, they simply want additional people encouraging them along the way.

Some come because they're on a search for answers. They want to ask questions about life's greatest mysteries. They desire a place to search alongside others. Here's the secret no one ever told me growing up. Churches are full of doubters, agnostics, and atheists. I hesitate to use those terms, though, because they don't fully embrace the complexity. I've known people who move back and forth between those categories in the course of one year. Many walk in the doors because they're haunted by a sense of transcendence. They want a group of people to do life with as they seek God and purpose. They don't want to be fed a bunch of shallow, easy answers.

No matter the reason one comes, the fact is that they do come. Every week, they come. Even as church attendance shrinks, people still come. Why? Because the church is there. Because it's accessible. Because no matter what happens in life, every seven days, it's Sunday.

This low bar for entry combined with consistent, open gatherings creates a fascinating petri dish of human community. By participating in church, I rub elbows with people whom I wouldn't be friends with if not for our church. We have different interests. We might vote differently. We come from different areas. At times, we interpret the Bible in different ways. Yet, we break bread every Sunday. We spend time together every single week, so we've become extremely tight. Frequency creates a type of bond that similarity cannot. Think about your life. While some of my community forms around common interest, most of my relationships form around accessibility and frequency. I know best those I know most.

The openness of church meetings leads to a radical inclusiveness. Specifically, the churches of my experience have shown an ability to not just tolerate but welcome weird people. I'm talking about awkward people. They speak in ways that violate cultural norms of interaction. I'm thinking of people who have lots of needs. I'm picturing the faces of friends who deserve an extra dose of patience. The church of my youth had so many of these people. In fact, church was the place where I encountered them the most. On TV and in media, everyone seemed cool. In school and sports, weird people often got pushed to the side. Even then, I realized how the elite avenues of society kept a tight guard on who got in. But with my church, I hung out with weird people. One day, as I contemplated this fact, I asked my second mom, "Why does our church have so many weird people?" Without missing a beat, I remember her saying, "Because that's who the church is. That's who Jesus spent time with. And by the way, be careful, some might think you're weird." Over time, I came to realize the beauty of all this weirdness. I came to appreciate the beauty of the odd, eclectic group assembled on Sundays.

From the earliest of times, the church brought together the outcasts of society, those thought of as weird. After all, Jesus ate with tax collectors and prostitutes. Others spent time with the haves, but Jesus spent time with the have-nots. Describing this dynamic, Jesus spoke these words in a parable in Luke 14:21: "Go out quickly into the streets and alleys of the town and bring in the poor, the crippled, the blind and the lame." The church, the Jesus movement, welcomed these people like no other social grouping. While other social groups had elaborate bars for entry, the church worked to have none. When you read Acts and Paul's letters, you may wonder about all the discussions on circumcision and food laws. It may not mean much to us, but it shows their desire to be an accessible community that clung to God's will. In this manner, the church became the most inclusive social group of the first century. I think back to my adolescent question, "Why are there so many weird people at church?" My heart may have been off, but I understood the nature of the church.

Growing up, when the topic of church attendance came up, the scripture often referred to was Hebrews 10:24–25. "And let us consider how we may spur one another on toward love and good deeds, not giving up meeting together, as some are in the habit of doing, but encouraging one another— and all the more as you see the Day approaching." While well intentioned, it often led to a "Go to church because the Bible says so." I now see that interpretation as flippant, shallow, and even unhelpful. It's not a command void of meaning or purpose. It's not a command merely for the sake of meeting a requirement. Why does the author tell them to meet? The purpose lies in encouraging each other. We don't show up for ourselves but for others. It's not about you or me. It's about others. Open, weekly gatherings depend on people showing up. Somewhere this Sunday, a lonely person searching for answers will walk through a church door. They'll push through any spiritual baggage they have or social phobias they experience. They'll walk in. When they do, someone will be there. You can count on that.

Some years ago, a middle-aged man named Elvis walked into our church. Due to some challenges beyond his control, he lives on a monthly government check. After paying rent, he has little left over. On the Sunday morning he first walked through our doors, he was hungry. I remember that Buford and Dot took him to Captain D's. Elvis kept coming back. At times, he behaves in ways divergent from normal social protocol. He likes talking about classic TV shows such as *Bonanza*. Since we've known him, he moves every six to twelve months. Early on, he decided my friend Matt was his favorite. Over the years, Matt has taken him to lunch several times a month as well as helped him when he needed a little extra support. Sometimes Elvis attends our church, and sometimes he attends one closer to where he lives. Still, our relationship with him continues. It's not one-sided, either. At times when my heart becomes hard, Elvis reminds me of key truths about God's love for each and every one of us. I'm thankful God brought Elvis our way.

We all have moments of pain and need when we want to reach out to someone. We need scheduled community with easy access. Every seven days is Sunday. On Sunday, you can walk into a Christian gathering and find community. There's no bar for entry. You can find consistent family. The church offers this.

12

Intergenerational Community

IN JULY OF 2002, Beth and I bought our first home. Married less than a year and in our early twenties, it felt overwhelming. I understood so little. I remember all the time I spent walking around the basement trying to wrap my mind around all the pipes, wires, and equipment. Suddenly, this was all ours, but I didn't know how to take care of it.

One huge benefit of getting our own place centered around having our own washer and dryer. I still remember the day that Lowes delivered the shiny new washer and dryer. I assured myself I knew how to hook it all up. After all, how hard could it be? They included an instruction manual. Within a few minutes, I got most of it hooked up right. Yet, one hose didn't quite seem to fit. I tried for about an hour as I twisted and turned it. Should I go back to the store? Maybe this was the wrong hose. I went back to the instruction book and the pile of parts on the floor.

Then, the doorbell rang. Relieved at the distraction, I went upstairs to find George and Elaine standing at our front door. Elaine held a plant. We smiled and invited them in. They were a married couple in their mid-sixties from our church. Apparently, they observed a custom of showing up at the door of new homeowners with a "housewarming" gift. Admittedly, this tradition was new to me, but I wasn't complaining. As Beth invited Elaine in for a conversation, George asked if he could help with anything. I invited him down to the basement. Once there, I showed him my predicament. He observed the scene for thirty seconds before saying, "Let me show you a trick." In short order, both the washer and dryer were up and running. George showed me how to do something he'd done many times before. He avoided condescension and gave me a sense of "We all go through this." George passed a skill down to me, a skill I didn't even know I needed an hour prior.

I'm fortunate to have experienced countless of these exchanges in my life. Because my parents surrounded me with a rich vibrant community of church, school, neighborhood, and youth sports, I knew many adults. This may seem like hopeless nostalgia to some, but I had a default sense of trust when it came to adults. I grew up in one of those environments where I had "uncles" and "aunts" who bore no blood relation. I grew up around countless adults who felt they had the green light to correct and encourage me.

Weekly, I witnessed healthy adults in most every generation of life, from young to old and everything in between. This intergenerational community gave me a script for what life could be. I never felt bound by this. Instead, I gravitated towards the numerous possibilities like grips on a rock-climbing wall. For many young people, the future offers a blank page. For me, I saw dozens of scripts, never a blank page. Many young people aspire to a certain type of "adult life" yet seem uncertain about the steps to get there. Surrounded by adults, I had a playbook.

I've witnessed and experienced this conversation too many times to count. A younger person, in late teens or early twenties, asks an older person in an ever-earnest voice, "How did you get to where you're at in life?" Normally, the older adult chuckles and talks about all the unplanned and unforeseen events of their life. Yet, eventually they'll say, "I did this, and then this happened. So I did this, and then this happened. So I did this, and then this happened." Conversations like this serve as the sharing of a life script. You don't have to follow the script, but wisdom leads one to learn all you can from it.

From the dawn of time, no doubt, tension has existed between generations. As we've probably all seen and perhaps even experienced, older generations can pressure the up-and-coming generation. They can give them one set script and actively work against any departure from that. Parent your kids this certain way. Do church this set way. Pursue your career like this. Personally, I don't find that desirable or healthy. However, I too often see another trend at work. Some in emerging generations reject being given any existing script. A positive spin might suggest they're charting their own way, but some might wonder if they're simply reinventing the wheel. When it came to George helping me with my washing machine, I saw no need to chart my own way. I simply wanted it to work. I eagerly accepted the given script.

Over the last year, in conversations with other men, I began to hear about a professor named Jordan Peterson. He wrote a bestseller entitled *12 Rules for Life* and packs venues around the country with fans eager to hear him. As I asked a friend for more details, I was told that the first rule is "Stand up straight with your shoulders back."[1] Peterson has spawned many reactions in recent years, and this was mine. Why did so many men need a book to tell them to "Stand up straight with your shoulders back"?

I never had to read that advice in a book because I grew up surrounded by people who stood up. Growing up, I was surrounded by men and women who stood up straight with shoulders back. Specifically, at my church, people dressed up, looked sharp, and walked in confidence. I practiced walking like them. As I've said throughout, they were far from perfect, and I spent time processing that as well. Still, I had scripts, and I practiced the various scripts.

I remember one particular gentleman who stood up straight, the elder from the church of my youth who ran a dairy. On occasion, he took kids from church to get a tour of the dairy. The tour often ended with chocolate milk or lemonade. He and his wife modeled elegance and grace, hospitality and generosity. They dressed nice but not fancy, classy but not showy. She regularly taught my Sunday school class and treated me like one of her own grandchildren. One year, our church did an official mentoring program. I hit the lottery in being paired with this gentleman. On one occasion, he and his wife, along with some of their friends, took me to see *Phantom of the Opera* at a downtown performance hall. My dad helped me get dressed for the night out. I remember wearing a sport coat. I was probably eleven or twelve years old, and I'm embarrassed to say I fell asleep during the musical. Even then, it embarrassed me. I remember thinking, "Stand up straight, offer a firm handshake, and look people in the eye. Act like him." I looked at his life, and I wanted a life like that. He gave me a possible script. I didn't need to read a book.

The prevailing script informally offered in my church took this shape: get baptized, graduate high school, figure out how to make college work, graduate college, get a job, find a spouse, be responsible, participate in a local church, take care of your business, invest in your community, love God and neighbor, have kids, learn to serve your local church, and then pass the

---

1. Peterson, *12 Rules for Life*, 1.

script on to your kids. Because of this, it's no surprise that my life took this shape. Sure, within the script, I took my own unique course. It was not a concrete mold but an elastic, flexible path. I'm grateful for that. I never felt pressure to take this path. I saw it around me, and it looked good. I freely chose it. Of course, as I ventured further into adulthood, I saw other experiences around me. I realized many hadn't been given the script. I realized many had the script cruelly forced on them. I realized many didn't even know a script existed.

Experience passed down from generation to generation makes us wiser. Sure, we swim in a sea of knowledge. But there lies a difference between knowledge and wisdom. We can have lots of information and options, but wisdom shows us how to use it. For example, I think back to my freshman year of college. I had a crush on a girl in one of my classes. I'd talked some with her, but I had trouble gauging her interest in going on a date. I couldn't tell if her responses constituted reciprocation or just politeness. It's an age-old question, right? How do I know if she's into me? Around this time, my roommate and I often ate Sunday lunch with a couple in their late sixties, Bob and Bernice. They'd known my roommate's parents' years before. We often attended worship with them and then rode over to their house.

After a few months and three to four lunches, I'd grown comfortable around them. Bob had advanced degrees in communication. He'd taught at the university level, worked internationally, and consulted with various corporations. He knew his stuff. So, at one particular lunch, I asked, "Mr. Bob, how do you know if a woman is interested in you? Is there a way to sense connection without embarrassing her or myself?" Bob took a deep breath, and I remember him saying, "Well, there's no foolproof way to read someone's mind, but yes, there are ways to assess connection." For close to an hour, he coached me on reading nonverbal cues as well as having direct yet nonconfrontational conversations. On top of that, he shared multiple stories to illustrate all of his points. I'll never forget it. It completely shaped how I handled relationships from then on.

Relationships across the generations give us these stories. Sadly though, we're often resistant to help from other age groups. Years later, while working with teens, I remembered this episode. I'd taken a group of teens on a weeklong trip. One night, I was driving a group of boys back to our housing. One boy uttered out, "No, that's not what I meant." I glanced in the rearview mirror. He was looking down at his phone. Apparently, he and his girlfriend had miscommunicated, and she was upset. Desperate to fix it, he kept trying to figure out what to text to her. His buddies all weighed in giving him advice on what to text. Knowing him well, I felt the space to wade in. "Call her, don't text her," I implored. "Text is not the ideal medium for conflict management. Reconciliation happens better over the phone. Face to face would be even better." He ignored me. His buddies gave embarrassingly bad advice. The miscommunication got worse and worse. "It's not working. Call her," I suggested again. "No," he said. "I got this." By the end of the night, she broke up with him.

These two anecdotes represent our options. We can engage the inherited wisdom of older generations, or we can ignore it all together. Too often, we do the latter. We coalesce around like-minded peer groups. In our time, we see immense generational tension amidst a widespread decline in generational engagement. Baby Boomers crack "Millennial" jokes. Younger folks groan about their old parents and their out of touch generation. Alongside all of this, we've witnessed a proliferation of generational identity analysis. Authors write bestsellers on understanding and connecting with various generations. What once seemed natural due to proximity now demands experts due to our social distance.

How did we get here? Certainly, we can point at many causes. Going back to the nineteenth century, the Industrial Revolution moved many families from rural farms to urban factories. Multiple generations had worked side by side on the farm but separated upon arriving in the city. Gradually, more and more families had two working parents. Well-intentioned child labor laws meant children had to be left at home. More and more children grew up in daycare, and education systems began earlier and extended later into life. On top of this, the busyness of modern life combined with the proliferation of entertainment options has shortened the amount of unstructured relational time that exists between generations. The end result is this: each generation mainly hangs out with itself. Younger generations especially find themselves in peer silos.

Likely, nothing shaped generational patterns as much as the embrace of age segregation in education. Early schoolhouses, out of necessity, no doubt, included various ages and levels. Over time, as education grew, kids of similar ages and skills were grouped together. Eventually, we came to our current system of grouping peers together all day long from ages five to eighteen. In the educational environment, kids interact with adults, but mostly in large settings with student-teacher ratios of 20:1. By the time kids graduate high school, they've been conditioned to form almost the entirety of their relationships around peers and a few family members.

For the last 150 years of American Christianity, church educational strategies have mirrored overall cultural educational strategies. Look no further than the idea of "Sunday school." Consider the modern church building. Many churches have a worship center (auditorium, sanctuary). Radiating out from this hub, you often find various wings such as "children's education," "youth education", and "adult education." Often, church buildings resemble school buildings and separate children into classes with one or two adults.

Even in the worship gathering, we've seen the vast expansion of age segregation in "children's church" and "youth worship." I've met teenagers who have never worshipped with their parents despite frequent church attendance. For many families in too many churches, they drive to worship together but say "Let's meet back here" as they each go their separate ways. Ironies abound in this approach. We focus on our families by separating them. We seek to mature our children by segregating them from mature adults. We teach our adults to love their kids by promising them they won't have to spend time with their kids on Sundays. Many church leaders worry that new families won't join their church if they have to sit with their own children. More than one adult has told me, "If my kids are with me, I don't get anything out of it."

I remember a conversation I had several years ago. One family had been worshipping with us for about six months. In a city full of churches, I asked why they'd landed with us. The answer came quickly. "Because you allow kids in worship." I recoiled and uttered, "Seriously, what do you mean?" He responded, "We got tired of the shoulder tap. At most churches, about five minutes into worship, you get a shoulder tap. A smiling adult whispers while looking at your children, 'We have a place for them to go.' They're nice about it. They may even think it's what is best, but they make it clear they want our kids elsewhere."

I remember a visit to another congregation a couple of years ago. Inside their bulletin, they included a statement like this: "We host a children's church for kids in the youth wing. You may check your child in at the welcome center. Disruptive children in the main worship service will be asked to leave so as not to distract the worship service." Clearly, if a small child runs and screams all over the place, they should at the very least be taken out momentarily to calm down. But the overall tone and message is crystal clear. We don't want your kids in here. Can you imagine how we'd react if we treated another demographic this way?

Age segregation has led to this Sunday dynamic for many churchgoing families. The family scatters into all corners of the church building. The family breaks apart to gather in generational silos. The church was always meant to be a haven of intergenerational relationship. Sadly, as culture became more and more segregated by age, the church followed.

Before charting the way back, we must face the consequences. First, age segregation has caused increasing estrangement between generations. No doubt, some generational tension occurs naturally. Looking around now, it appears worse than years passed. More and more, we see churches with one major generational demographic. We have Millennial churches or Generation X churches or Baby Boomer churches. I've even seen older generations plant and fund a church plant for a different generation. It's easier to start and pay for it than bridge the generational gap.

I believe kids who grow up in age segregated congregations harbor a "This is not for me because it was never mine." Many have shared with me an innate feeling of otherness stemming from their days of being pushed to the side. Of course, this breaks the hearts of adults who labored to produce these generational programs. They worked and prayed to do what was best. How can a kid who grew up in a church youth wing with carefully painted walls, flat-screen TVs, gyms, and playgrounds feel cheated? These were great hospitable loving programs. It was all well-intentioned but disconnected. Generations cannot take a baton that was never handed to them. I can't help but wonder. It's not quitting if it was never yours to begin with.

Second, age segregation caused widespread juvenilization in both culture at large and Christianity in particular. When generations cling together and spend the majority of time around peers, they normalize their coming-of-age style and behavior. The fashions of youth become enshrined in their thinking. Separated from consistent, close relationships with adults, they miss out on some of the major factors which cause maturation, namely, time with those who you want to become. This type of pattern brings a cyclical effect. As each generation solidifies the fashions of youth into their generational mantra for life, it creates an absence of true adulthood.

Consider the mainstream American church dynamic for teenagers since the 1970s. An increased focus on separating teens out for pizza, games, and devotionals catered to a specific set of ideals. The emphasis on doctrine, Bible, and creeds declined as the emphasis on high-octane activities, relational connections with peers, and "my relationship with Jesus" increased. Faith came alive and relevant for many in a personal way, yet it often lacked mature roots into the depth of Christian themes.

To reverse the trends of juvenilization, churches must recapture the original Christian vision of intergenerational churches. Our culture shows no signs of ending age segregation as well as its associated immaturity. This shift will truly be countercultural. Moreover, for those accustomed to the age segregation church strategies of the past fifty years, this may even seem like a step back.

Perhaps we need fresh ears to hear the words of Jesus. In the Gospels, the apostles tried to enforce age segregation around Jesus. His response in Matthew 19:14 leaves no room for interpretation or doubt. "Let the little children come to me, and do not hinder them, for the kingdom of heaven belongs to such as these." Jesus wanted to spend time with children. Jesus wanted adults to spend time with children. This scripture offers the theological foundation for bringing the generations together.

In like manner, in 1 Timothy 5:1–2, Paul offers direct teaching on treating the adults in the church as family members. "Do not rebuke an older man harshly but exhort him as if he were your father. Treat younger men as brothers, older women as mothers, and younger women as sisters, with absolute purity." It's tempting to see all the honorary "uncles" and "aunts" of my childhood as a folksy Southern relic. It's tempting to see the Sunday greeting to "brother" and "sister" as pious church talk. But, when I consider these biblical commands, I see the purpose of God. The church is family, a family made up of many ages put together for a reason.

So, how can we recapture and embrace the intergenerational intention of the local church? First off, I don't believe we should immediately cancel all of our age-specific programming or repurpose the youth spaces in our church buildings. Knee-jerk reactions will create more confusion than healthy change and needed consensus. Second, the beauty of this likely lays in relational emphasis and tone, not the structuring of programs. An initial step centers on getting more adults in student programs as well as asking people to take a generational inventory of their relationships. If all relationships center on their age demographic, an adjustment in focus may be needed. Third, I have no desire to imply that age-specific programming always represents a shortcoming. At times, it's good and needed. Instead, I'm suggesting we change our default setting. For many, age-specific programming is the default. I hope to see a day when combined intergenerational settings, especially in worship, are the default. We would break into age specific groups as an exception, not the rule.

What does this look like in practice? Growing up, I went through a stage where I really liked watching war movies. After a childhood of G.I. Joe comic books, I graduated into watching movies on World War II, Korea, and Vietnam. I liked the fighting. I gloried in the triumph. One Sunday after worship, I told some buddies I'd watched the movie *Platoon* the night before. Part of me thought it was really cool, even as it raised troubling questions for me. Part of me just thought I was supposed to see it as cool. Apparently, Tommy, my youth minister, overheard this conversation. The next week, he brought in another gentleman, Gerald, to teach the class. Gerald had served in Vietnam. In age-appropriate ways, he told us about war. He shared the nightmares he still had, as well as the friends he lost. All of this conversation took place in a spiritual atmosphere. I've never watched a war movie the same way again. My buddies and I needed a gentle nudge out of our immature views on war. These men gave it to us.

Back in those days, my church culture talked often about fighting temptation. On one occasion, Tommy talked about his struggles with pornographic magazines years prior as a young adult. He told stories about the secrecy involved as well as the ways shame kept him down. He spoke directly to the importance of confession and the way it breaks temptation's power. As a teenager, I frequently heard adult men share their struggles with temptation, whether it be pornography, drugs and alcohol, gambling, or anger. This taught me to refrain from putting humans on pedestals. This taught me to expect temptation, so I didn't freak out when it happened to me. Their stories and testimonies gave me an arsenal of weapons for my own spiritual battles.

When my father came to faith as a teenager, he received an intergenerational community from his church. Specifically, he had a friend who played a big brother role to him, Tommy (another Tommy). He was five or six years older than my dad. He coached him on getting and keeping jobs. He offered advice on college and educational pursuits. Tommy even sent him a little spending money while my dad was in college. Tommy was always just a little ahead of my dad on the "road of life." Therefore, he had a knack for being able to share with my dad what to expect. Dad appreciated this and relished the wisdom he received from Tommy. Looking back now, I see the way my dad always sought to be like Tommy to other younger men.

Years ago, I chatted with three high school seniors in my church. In the course of the conversation, I asked them about their intended major in college. All three said they wanted to be engineers. "Oh," I replied, "That's a great major. Have you ever talked to an engineer about what they do? Do you know any engineers?" They admitted they'd never actually talked to an engineer. "Would you like to?" I asked. Within the month, I organized a brief sit-down with them and several engineers from our congregation. None of it was difficult or earth shattering. Yet, it shows our default posture of age segregation. None of the high school students had considered sharing their vocational plan with an adult in that same vocation. None of the adults had considered reaching out to any of the teens who might want to join their vocation.

As a last story, I remember a men's retreat years ago. Robert, one of our elders, was set to speak on the second night of the event. As he tried to discern between several topics, he asked my opinion about what he should say. I encouraged him to talk about his life and share some successes and failures. "Oh," he said, "they don't want to hear about my struggles." "Oh," I replied, "I think they do. We want to learn from you guys but don't know how to ask." That night, he shared some incredibly vulnerable stories of amazing highs and desperate lows. You could have heard a pin drop. Younger men sat on the edge of their seats. Robert wove it all back to Jesus and biblical virtues. Afterwards, young men asked him questions until late in the night. The wisdom flow didn't just go one direction, though. Sure, the younger men learned from Robert, but he learned from them as well. Talking to him the next week, he joyfully shared new insights and reflections he had from hearing their stories. It goes both ways. Old learn from the young, and young learn from the old. We crave this type of thing but struggle to pursue it.

So what do you do when you can't figure out how to hook up your washing machine? Do you want to have older and younger people in your life? Do you want your kids to have older mentors? Do you want an intergenerational community? In a world segregated by age, church just may be the best place to find it. In an increasingly knowledgeable but immature world, we need other generations more than ever.

Parenting kids in this world can be overwhelming. As a parent, I often feel like I need help, so much help. I've read a lot of ideas on providing a broad framework of social support for our kids. I've explored mentoring strategies. I've seen how some families look for programs to give their child a boost, and some of these plans no doubt have a lot to offer. But I'm not looking for a program. I'm overwhelmed as a parent, but I already have a strategy. It's called church. I'm gonna involve my kids in a church, the best and maybe last place to find intergenerational community.

What do you want for your kids and grandkids? How will they find a script, a map of possibilities? Too often, society wants to separate the generations and pit us against each other. There's a better way. Jesus says let the little children come. In the church, Jesus gets his way. You can do life with other generations. We can all learn from each other and support each other. The church offers this.

13

Transnational Identity

GROWING UP, EVERY SO often, my grandparents spoke French. English was their native tongue, but they learned French during the two years they lived in French West Africa, specifically Abidjan, Cote d'Ivoire. They loved to pull out old maps, photos, and carvings from that time of their life. Then, they'd dazzle me by breaking into conversation in French. I remember a trip with them to Quebec. Gramps couldn't wait to practice his French. From the looks on the faces of locals, I think he was a tad rusty, but they appreciated his effort.

Languages fascinate me and always have. As a kid, I'd ask my parents and grandparents, "Why don't we all speak the same language? Where did languages come from?" In response, they told me one of the ancient human origin stories, found in Genesis 11. On the plains of Shinar, a group of people sought to build a tower to "make a name for ourselves." We read what happens next in Genesis 11:6–9:

> The Lord said, "If as one people speaking the same language they have begun to do this, then nothing they plan to do will be impossible for them. Come, let us go down and confuse their language so they will not understand each other." So the Lord scattered them from there over all the earth, and they stopped building the city. That is why it was called Babel—because there the Lord confused the language of the whole world. From there the Lord scattered them over the face of the whole earth.

That story mesmerized me. As I grew older, I often wanted to "make a name for myself." Even more, I wanted to be a part of something greater than myself. Sometimes, this drive led to beauty. Sometimes, it led to vain hubris. As social media became a reality, I saw the universal drive to "make a name for ourselves" even clearer. Sometimes, it's led to beauty. Other times, it's led to confusion. I often think of the Babel story. I believe it offers us a truth. We want to be a part of something larger than ourselves.

In the spring of 1993, my Spanish teacher took a group of students from my high school on a trip to Mexico. I'd looked forward to this trip for a long time. When I first expressed interest, my parents said they'd pay half, but I had to work and save up the other half. As you might imagine, that personal investment deepened both my anticipation and engagement for the trip. My Spanish class took on greater meaning, and I looked forward to communicating outside English for the first time.

The trip did not disappoint. We flew to Mexico City, and I eagerly tried to read all the signs in Spanish. For the first time, I experienced a type of cultural immersion where I felt like the proverbial other. Within, I felt a mild angst. I was a stranger in a strange land. I stood out. Yet, every Mexican I encountered greeted me with gracious hospitality. I especially remember our trip out to Teotihuacan to see the Aztec pyramids. I struck up a conversation with our bus driver. I happened to wear a Los Angeles Dodgers hat that day, and he wanted to talk about Fernando Valenzuela, the talented Dodgers pitcher from Mexico who led them to the 1981 World Series title. As we talked baseball, I felt the joy that we humans feel when we cross cultural differences to experience the joy of commonality. The "us" and "them" dichotomies fall away. Strangers become friends.

After a couple of days in Mexico City, we took a bus trip south to Acapulco, where we'd later fly out. We stopped for the night in a mountain town named Taxco. Feeling a bit stir-crazy after several days of organized tours and bus rides, I desperately wanted to get out and do something on my own. A few blocks up a hill from our hotel, some buddies and I found a concrete sports field. It offered both soccer goals and basketball hoops. A group of teens and twentysomethings were playing soccer. "Podemos jugar?" Can we play? Graciously, they allowed us to join them. Looking back, I can't remember whose idea it was, but we played against them. We didn't form a line and pick teams or blend in with their existing teams. It was us against them, Mexico vs. U.S.A. I bet you can guess what happened next. They destroyed us. Few of us had played much soccer, and they immediately feasted on fresh meat. Quickly, I grew frustrated. I hadn't been able to run or play in days, and now I found myself getting whooped in a sport I cared little about at the time.

After half an hour or so of a beatdown, we got an idea. We picked up a basketball in the corner and gestured towards the hoop. They nodded, and we changed sports. You can likely guess what happened next. The tables had turned. We destroyed them. Honestly, I played as hard as I'd ever played. As we developed a lead, I did not let up. Sadly, after half an hour of this, tempers began to flare. I can't remember all the details, but probably someone fouled someone a bit too hard. One of the Mexicans turned to us, and in his best English he let loose a strong and pointed curse word. One of my American buddies straightened his back and in his best Spanish translated the curse word right back at him. At that point, both groups decided it was best to call it a night before tempers flared even more. As we jogged back to our hotel, I remember chanting, "USA, USA." I felt a jolt of energy, a rush of adrenaline, in that experience. I felt very American, and it felt good.

The following summer, I had a very different type of experience. I traveled with my church to Tegucigalpa, Honduras. Many of the adults worked as nurses, doctors, or dentists. We visited a faith-based medical clinic. The clinic had regular healthcare providers, but during the summer, groups from America would come and see an increased number of patients. Along with the other teens in the group, our job centered on playing with the kids during the day in the field beside the clinic. We did skits of Bible stories and sang songs. At this point, my two years of high school Spanish had become really helpful. At lunch time, we made tons of peanut butter sandwiches. After all of that, we still had plenty of time to kill. So, as you might expect, we played lots of soccer. Not surprisingly, my soccer skills had not improved. But on this trip, we didn't play us versus them. We played together. I played hard. I tried to win, yet I didn't become frustrated. I felt a great sense of peace.

Over the next couple of summers, I went back to Honduras. Once again, I spent the week playing with the kids, while they and their parents waited to see the nurses, doctors, and dentists. My older brother and I grew close with two other brothers, Honduran boys named Eduardo and Manny. They were only a few years younger than us. During the days, we spent considerable time talking. We worked on our Spanish, and they worked on their English. We shared stories about our lives and drank lots of Kool-Aid. At the end of each trip, we'd say goodbye. These partings grew more and more emotional with each passing year. I never knew what to say. As I went back each summer, I began to ask more and more questions about poverty, immigration, and best practices for mission work. At the time, I had few answers—not that I have all the answers now—and plenty of confusion. So, as I said goodbye, I offered the only parting phrases I knew from Spanish class. "Que Dios le Bendiga"—God bless you. "Vaya con Dios"—Go with God. Then, I'd get on the bus and walk to the back. Out of the corner of my eye, I'd look at my brother. He was crying. I never saw him cry, but he cried then.

These experiences forced me to ask deep questions about faith and politics. Growing up, both patriotism and religion surrounded me. In my elementary school, we opened every school day with the Pledge of Allegiance and a prayer. One year, sometime in the mid-1980s, the annual school play focused on American history. It culminated with a guest appearance by Lee Greenwood, who sang "God Bless the U.S.A." All of this converged in my mind. I pictured a red, white, and blue Jesus who died to give us salvation, freedom, and the right to be Americans.

Growing up in the 1980s during the late stages of the Cold War and Iron Curtain, I feared communism and the atheism often associated with it. The church of my youth constantly spoke of evangelism and sharing the gospel. Taken together, I came to see the United States as the center and vanguard of Christianity. The lots of America and the Christian faith seemed fused together. To root for the country was to spread the faith. I saw little if any separation in the two. I brought a similar intensity of focus during Sunday Communion and the national anthem.

To be clear, I never remember being taught this. Instead, these were the childlike assumptions I made based on the indirect messages of my environment. Looking back, I'm confident my family, mentors, and teachers valued the kingdom of God more than the United States. Still, I think fears ranging from communism to secularism to the culture wars brought about an unhealthy merger of spiritual fervor and patriotism. Allow me to be up front. I'm thankful for the United States. I'm thankful to be an American and to have grown up in the country. Still, it's not the kingdom of God. We must be clear about that. Frequently, politicians from both major parties use messianic-type language for their leaders. I support good governance. We need it, but we must caution expectations and guard against misplaced trust. We can respect and honor our country without regarding it as the kingdom.

Many like to talk about Christian America. Many like to talk about a nation founded on Christian principles. To be sure, the majority of those who founded the country identified as Christians. Still, in our common folklore, we almost picture them as daily Bible-reading, Sunday school heroes. In contrast, many of the founding fathers and mothers were not regular churchgoers. Many espoused forms of deism and rejected the miraculous parts of the Bible. Most historians believe a much higher percentage of Americans attend church today than in the late eighteenth century.[1]

I don't mean to doubt the good done by the founding fathers and mothers, but an honest assessment of their religiosity makes their shortcomings easier to process. After all, deep sexism and racism show up in our founding attitudes. I gravitate to this reflection from Frederick Douglass: "I can see no reason, but the most deceitful one, for calling the religion of this land Christianity." Clearly, his social experience and location allowed him to see gaps between the teachings of Jesus and American practice. If we recognize and acknowledge this, we can admit that America has not always done the will of God. Perhaps, America began as a nation largely numbered by those who identified as Christians, but that doesn't mean America began on the teachings of Christ.

Once again, my goal does not lie in ridiculing the United States. No nation has consistently followed the teachings of Christ. This harsh reality frees us from ultimate allegiance to the nation-state and into dependence on the kingdom of God. Before we can experience the multinational kingdom of God, we must crucify the notion that one nation has a monopoly on Christian faithfulness.

Once, on the way home from school, one of my daughters began a conversation this way. "Dad, the Pledge of Allegiance is creepy." Parents frequently experience surprising conversations, but this caught me off guard. I decided to put it back on her. "Why is it creepy?" She thought for a second. "Well, they make us do it. We have to put our hands over our heart. And, it seems like a prayer. It just feels creepy to me." Now, while I think a bit of patriotism can be good in healthy ways, I sensed she was on to something. She loves history and eagerly consumes stories about the nation. Still, when devotion to the nation began to resemble and even overpowered devotion to Jesus, she reacted with a "This is creepy." She's on to something. Perhaps, more of us need to reflect on how patriotism can slowly compete for our highest loyalty if we're not aware.

From my childhood until now, I've always enjoyed watching the Olympics. I like the blend of healthy patriotism and global unity. Throughout my life, watching the Olympics has been an overt time of rooting for my

1. Black, *Beyond Left and Right*, 58–59.

country. While I normally follow major American sports like baseball, basketball, and football, I will watch sports ranging from badminton to cycling with this catch. I want to have an American for whom to root. If there's an American, if there's a chance for "us" to win, I'm in.

However, on a few occasions, the following happened. As you know, the TV networks have a great way of showing behind the scenes to personalize the athletes. Often, I get caught up in the backstory. At times, I'd read a lot about different athletes and their personal journeys. On several occasions, I read about the devout faith practice of an athlete from a different country. In these moments, I felt torn. Do I root for the American without a compelling story or the non-American with the touching story? Do I root for the secular American or the non-American Christian? At times, I rooted for the non-American Christian, even as they competed against an American. That felt different, yet right.

Deep down, this is really all just a reflection on identity. When we look in the mirror, what do we see? Do we see an American or a Christian? Clearly, one can be both. But what is first? In the deepest part of our being, who are we? What is the fundamental source of my identity: male, white, father, husband, friend, American, or Christian? For the disciple of Jesus, there's only one answer. Yet, other identities creep in and often claim supremacy. The healthiest way to discern our hearts on this lies in spending time with other Christians around the world.

In the mid-1990s, on one of my trips to Honduras, my youth minister, Tommy, took us to a life-changing worship service. Each Sunday, a local Honduran minister traveled to the men's prison in Tegucigalpa. He led a Christian worship service, including the sharing of the Lord's Supper. On this Sunday, he extended the invitation to our visiting group. Several of the men wanted to go, and Tommy invited some of the older teen boys including me. This made me nervous. Prison, especially a foreign prison, made my heart race. However, I felt I needed to go.

I remember going through security. I remember hearing the ominous sound of the door locking behind me. I remember walking through a cold courtyard. Then I remember walking into a crowded room full of warmth. I was unprepared for the welcome awaiting us. Prisoners greeted us with smiles and handshakes. I could follow bits and pieces of the service, but I confess I couldn't discern the thrust of the sermon. However, as the service grew towards its climax, we left the limits of Spanish and English behind. The minister stood at the front of the room and held up a large cracker.

He closed his hands in reverent, fervent prayer, and then he broke it. Suddenly, the men in the room ceased to be strangers and became brothers. We weren't Americans or Hondurans, primarily. We were disciples of Christ.

Now, I realize how that may sound. It's easy for me to say. I got on a plane later that week and went back to a prosperous nation and good life. I don't remember any names from that decades-old experience. I don't know if the men received just or unjust sentences. I get it. This experience cost me nothing. But it did change me. As I walked out of prison that morning, I knew there was something more than language or country. Something greater existed, and I wanted to be part of that.

Christ did not come for one language or nation. Christ came to unite all in the language of the Spirit and form a transnational kingdom. In Genesis 12, God chose Abraham. He promised he'd turn him into a great nation. However, the purpose of choosing one nation never centered on nationalism. God told Abraham in Genesis 12:3, "all peoples on earth will be blessed through you." God desired Israel to be a "light to nations" in Isaiah 51:4. The prophets did not see Jerusalem as a location of national supremacy but as a future blessing to all nations. As both Isaiah and Micah proclaimed in Isaiah 2:2 and Micah 4:1, "all nations will stream to Zion." We clearly see this direction in Jesus, who welcomed and embraced Samaritans. In Acts 10:34–35, we clearly see this in Peter, who proclaimed, "I now realize how true it is that God does not show favoritism but accepts from every nation the one who fears him and does what is right." If the transnational identity goes over our head in all of this, John's words in Revelation 7:9–10 make it crystal clear.

> After this I looked, and there before me was a great multitude that no one could count, from every nation, tribe, people and language, standing before the throne and before the Lamb. They were wearing white robes and were holding palm branches in their hands. And they cried out in a loud voice: "Salvation belongs to our God, who sits on the throne, and to the Lamb."

Do we believe this? Do we practice this? Do we picture a national or transnational heaven? If the latter, do we live into that now?

Perhaps, there's never been a more important time to embrace this. Our world struggles and festers under the challenge of local allegiance and global partnership. Globalism has brought us a mixed bag. Many have benefitted, and many have been left behind. In response, as humanity has often done, we see a tendency to retreat back into one's own country, region, and group. It's a dizzying landscape, full of finger-pointing and scapegoating. Fear reigns. That's why transnational identity proves so important for the disciple. It enables us to process and navigate these times. Our story does not center on building a nation but on immersing ourselves in the kingdom.

I'm reminded of my first trip to the United Kingdom in 2007. I took some university students to do some community work with a local church over their spring break. A gracious group of hosts opened up their homes and lives for that week. One night, we all went out to dinner at an Italian restaurant. One of the local Christians volunteered at a nearby university where he mentored international students. So on this night, a group representing China, the United Kingdom, and the United States ate Italian cuisine together.

For almost two hours, I talked with two students from China. After the normal pleasantries, we began to ask about each other's countries of origin. They patiently and kindly told me about China and corrected some of my lack of understanding. Then, they told me they had two questions about America. Remember it was 2007. Question number one: "Why does every American have so many guns?" Question number two: "Why are all the housewives so desperate?" That last question made me laugh, as I recognized they'd been watching *Desperate Housewives*. I assured them that most housewives didn't share that level of desperation. I acknowledged that many have guns, but it's still not quite like the movies.

Here's what stuck out to me in the conversation. In many ways, these two students associated the Christian faith with America. Therefore, they saw the behavior depicted in movies as Christian values and behavior. This experience, and many others before and after, reminded me that the United States and its culture falls far short of the kingdom of God. We must proclaim and live into the transnational identity of the kingdom of God. We can still be good citizens of our particular country, but we must clearly distinguish between what's primary and secondary.

Scripture reminds us in Isaiah 40:8 that "the grass withers and the flowers fall, but the word of our God endures forever." In Matthew 16:18, Jesus proclaimed, "I will build my church, and the gates of hell shall not prevail against it." The same cannot be said about any one nation, even the United States. For several years now, I've said this out loud to students and local churches. "The United States will not last forever, but the kingdom of God will last forever." I've noticed a fascinating dynamic when I say this. Ears prick up. Daydreamers come to. Distracted kids suddenly pay attention. It sounds like heresy, yet it has the ring of truth. I'm thankful to be a citizen of the United States, and I believe the country has done much good. However, we must get accustomed to the idea that it will not last forever. When I read the end of Revelation about the New Heavens and the New Earth, I don't see the United States or any other nation. We must say this out loud until it no longer sounds like heresy but resonates in our gut for the truth it is.

In May of 2017, my family took some university students on a trip to Italy. It represented our first family experience with jet lag. We landed in Rome one morning, and we couldn't check in to our hotel until the afternoon. We went with the strategy of trying to stay up until evening. With no room, we wandered the streets. I could sense the culture shock in my children. For the first time in their lives, they were a cultural minority. Everything around was new and different to them. They were strangers in a strange land. As we wandered the streets of Rome, we passed a church. We ventured in to be received with great welcome. We found an empty pew and rested our weary, jet-lagged legs. As we looked around, we saw familiarity. In the center of the sanctuary stood the most familiar of all symbols, a large cross. On the stained glass windows, the girls saw the stories they'd heard their entire life, stories from Scripture. In an unfamiliar land, they saw the familiar faces of Mary, Joseph, John, Moses, and of course Jesus. In a land of an unfamiliar language, they heard the familiar language of the Spirit. Jet-lagged and weary, we were among our people. The look on their faces told quite a story. They were realizing the enormity of the kingdom of God. The language was different. The food was different. The culture was different. But Jesus was the same, all over the world.

In my teaching, I often meet students with roots in other countries. Some have come here specifically to study. Others are first- or second-generation immigrants. Frequently, my most impactful teacher-student relationships happen among them. Particularly, I've relished my time with Egyptian students, most of whom identify as Coptic Christians. Several have taken classes from both me and my wife. Some have gone on trips with us. You may remember this tragedy in February of 2015. ISIS marched twenty-one Egyptian Coptic Christians in Libya to the beach. Then, as they filmed a carefully constructed propaganda video, they executed them all.

As soon as I heard, I emailed two of my Coptic students. Certainly, this tragedy would have moved me even if I knew no Egyptians. Due to my relationships, though, I felt it. It felt personal. I conveyed my sorrow and grief to them. I tried to express my solidarity with them. Some weeks later, they invited me to their Good Friday service. Flattered at the invitation, I enthusiastically agreed. While the service occurred in Arabic, they projected the English translation onto the wall. However, I rarely looked at the English translation. A few minutes in, I realized it wasn't necessary to understand the service. I didn't need to know Arabic to understand their passion, zeal, and love for the Lord Jesus.

Sitting there amidst an unfamiliar tongue, I had moments when it felt like Babel. But honestly, after a while, it felt more like Pentecost. On the Pentecost of old, the Spirit came down and everyone heard the gospel in their own langue. The unity of Pentecost brought together the disrupted discord of Babel. At that Good Friday service, I couldn't interpret everything going on, but I could hear the Spirit. In their hospitality, care for each other, and reverent worship, I felt at home. These were my people. I had a family larger than any one nation. I'm part of something bigger than myself, bigger than my country. The church offers this.

14

Ethical Transformation

YEARS AGO, WHILE IN college, I began flexing my independence muscles. Like many in their early twenties, I played with my personality and tried on some new ways of being myself. Miles and miles away from people who knew me as a child and teen, I made some changes. Some of these were good. Some not so much. I grew more confident socially, but I also got a little cocky. I quit caring so much about what people thought, which was good in some ways. However, at times, I didn't care as much about how my behavior affected others. I began to approach individuals and groups based on what I could get out of them and didn't consider what might be best for them. Specifically, I began handling social relationships, both friendships and dating relationships, in an arrogant, calloused way. Quite honestly, I was full of myself.

Those college years proved so unique because no one there knew me prior, except one. One of my best friends, Travis, had gone to college with me. We roomed together every year of college except one, our junior year. It happened to be this particular year that my behavior veered off into extreme selfishness. One day, I remember he came over to my apartment to hang out for a few minutes. Eventually, the conversation turned to various things we'd both been up to. As I recounted the previous week, he got quiet. Sensing his disapproval, in a frustrated tone, I told him, "There's nothing wrong with what I'm doing." Here's what I meant by that. This is what college students do. I'm not doing anything unusual. Honestly, I wasn't doing anything crazy. I wasn't directly hurting anyone. I was just doing what I wanted to do without worrying so much about how it affected others. I'll never forget his answer to my defensive, "I'm not doing anything wrong." He paused and simply said, "Yeah, but you're better than that."

His words smacked me right between the eyes. "You're better than that." I knew he was right. I could try to rationalize my behavior all I wanted, but I knew he was right. I was called to be better. This selfishness wasn't good for me or anyone else. There were consequences. That very day, I began making changes. I leaned into his words. Within months, I met the woman who would eventually become my wife and the mother of my three children. I can tell you this. If I'd been acting as narcissistic as I had my junior year, she wouldn't have been interested in me. While my selfishness remains a work in progress, that junior year probably stands out as the low point. I needed someone to get in my face a bit. Because Travis did, my life turned out very differently.

Do you have people who speak truth to you? Are you surrounded by people who love you enough to tell you when you're wrong? Specifically, if you have unethical or immoral habits, do you have anyone in your life who will make you better? Do you have anyone in your life who loves you enough to have hard, difficult conversations?

We struggle with these conversations, don't we? Confrontation takes energy. It's messy. The path of least resistance remains far easier. If people don't take kindly to our well-intentioned critique, they might lash out. Confrontation can bring consequences with it. Deep down, we want to be liked. If we name bad behavior in others, they probably won't like us as much. There's a risk to it. On top of that, it doesn't seem nice to say hard things. None of us wake up wanting critique. In this way, it becomes a perverse golden rule. We don't want to hear challenging things, so let's not challenge others. We think this is love, even as lack of confrontation hurts others and ourselves.

Malcolm Gladwell writes about this in the seventh chapter of his 2008 book, *The Outliers*.[1] In the late 1990s, Korean Air had a much higher level of plane crashes than other airlines of comparable size. Understandably, this might lead one to wonder about the quality of the airplanes. However, Gladwell points the blame in another direction. In his view, the hierarchal nature of the pilot-copilot relationship kept copilots from confronting their pilots. Using the flight logs, he weaves a story ripe with failures to confront. The copilot didn't feel freedom to point out mistakes for fear of retaliation

---

1. Gladwell, *Outliers*, 177.

and bucking the system. The result was quite disastrous for all involved. When we don't challenge one another, we all suffer.

When we don't confront, we feign love, respect, and being nice. As it turns out, though, a refusal to speak up might be the most unloving thing one can do. The other day at worship, I had something on my face. As I remember, it was a piece of tissue that got stuck on my face after blowing my nose in the restroom. Likely, as I greeted folks prior to service, around twenty to twenty-five people saw the tissue on my face. However, only one person, a teen guy named Aiden, told me. When I said, "Good morning Aiden," he calmly responded. "Good morning J.P. You have something on your face." He didn't make it weird. He was neither angry nor apologetic. He just stated a fact, and I appreciated it. I wondered why others hadn't done it before him.

A couple of years ago, as I approached forty, I wanted to do a triathlon for the first time. So, I entered the local sprint marathon. I would need to swim for three hundred meters, bike for twenty-two kilometers, and run for five kilometers. The first two events intimidated me, since I had little to no experience. At first, I went to the pool alone and tried to figure it out. Quickly, I realized the rusty state of my strokes as well as my inability to breathe efficiently. In response, I talked to my friends who regularly swim. They suggested videos, which I watched multiple times. Eventually, I took four swim lessons at the YMCA. At first, I felt a tinge of embarrassment. After all, I knew how to swim. Brad, a buddy of mine, saw me one day and asked what I was doing with a confused look. Yes, I knew how to swim, but I had to confess that I didn't swim well. I needed help. Biking proved similar. When I did the stationary bike at the YMCA, I got really bored and had trouble knowing how to pace myself. So, I joined a spin class. Surrounded by others and led by a teacher, I biked faster and harder than ever before.

Accountability works. Allowing others to confront you, in speech or example, will make you better. We know this when it comes to fitness and sports. We know this when it comes to music and theater. We know this when it comes to education and work. Oddly though, we forget this when it comes to morality. To become a more ethical person, you need the loving confrontation that comes from a culture of accountability. Where do you find this, though? Sure, you can easily find exercise classes and acting classes. You can find computer and foreign language classes. Where do you find morality classes though? Where do we find ethical accountability?

For centuries, religious communities have existed as the centerpiece of behavioral accountability. Churches focused on ethical teaching and encouragement. Certainly, hypocrisy has had a long life in the church and elsewhere. Still, by and large, forming moral behavior loomed as a chief hope and goal of congregational life. People joined churches to get their lives right and stay right. Positive peer pressure emerges and sometimes even leads to face-to-face confrontation.

We don't do this as much anymore, for a few reasons. First, in America, rampant individualism leads to a widespread mantra of "Mind your own business" even in church. We see little difference between "Get off my lawn" and "Get out of my ethics." Second, the emphasis on "justification by grace through faith" in Protestant circles sometimes has led to the maximation of belief alongside the minimization of behavior. I affirm the emphasis on grace and faith, but I long for the biblical sequence of works flowing out of faith. As James 2:17 says, "faith without works is dead." You may have seen the bumper sticker, "not perfect, just forgiven." When these cars swerve into my lane while checking their phone, I can't help but think, "I'm not expecting perfection, but can you try a little harder?" Third, many of us fear that moral accountability will drive people away. The consumerist trends mentioned previously rarely mesh well with behavioral confrontation. People want comfortable religious programming, not challenging ethical work outs.

As the church has concentrated on this less and less, we've seen other groups lead the way. I'm constantly in awe of Alcoholics Anonymous and Narcotics Anonymous. They know the possibility of consistent, long-term change demands accountability. They're not afraid to be realistic about the challenging steps it takes to truly change. Years ago, one of my friends became dependent on prescription drugs and ultimately fell into drug abuse. In the midst of a month-long stay at a rehabilitation facility, I went to visit him. After a time of listening and encouraging him, I asked him, "What's the plan? How can you maintain this positive change once you leave here?" His answer caught me off guard. "I'm gonna do ninety meetings in ninety days." This sounded extreme to me. It felt daunting. Over time, I found this to be a frequent refrain. "Ninety meetings in ninety days." To maintain difficult change, we need daily accountability. We can't take days off. Because he heeded this refrain, he's found success living in freedom. It would not have happened without a group committed to the process of ethical change and unafraid of the route it takes to get there.

Throughout history, the church has offered this space. In many places, it still does, even as we should seek improvement. What does this path look like? First, we must embrace the time-honored truth that transformation can happen through Jesus. We can change. We can be better than we are now. While some peculiarities of our personality may haunt us for years, we can improve. The belief in change offers one of the bedrocks of the Christian faith. As Paul says in 2 Corinthians 5:17, "If anyone is in Christ, the new creation has come. The old has gone. The new is here." You can be new.

Growing up, I saw this firsthand. In my years without a mom, my father often grew impatient. With the benefit of maturity and hindsight, I can now understand why. Being a single parent is really, really hard. He courageously juggled many plates, but at times it got the best of him. I was a messy kid. You don't even want to know how much toothpaste I got on a sink, even the walls at times. Every now and then, Dad would raise his voice at me and my brother. He didn't scream. He was never abusive. But he did raise his voice, and none of us, including him, really liked that.

Most every night before bed, we sat in a sofa chair which we lovingly referred to as "the orange chair." Picture a late-1970s orange. My older brother and I would sit on each arm of the chair while Dad sat in the middle. He'd read us a Bible story, and then we'd pray together. I remember him saying this on more than one occasion. "Boys, I'm sorry I keep raising my voice. We're gonna ask God to help me not raise my voice." It was a real simple, yet honest prayer. Over time, it worked. Dad raised his voice less and less. Years later, I can't even remember the last time I saw him lose his patience. When I tell this story to those who know him, they can't believe it. Now, we all regard him as one of the most patient people we know. How did he make this change? God transformed him through prayer and accountability.

Change is possible. When people excuse bad behavior by saying, "That's just how they are," I get frustrated. While we'll likely never completely conquer temptation, we can be better than we are now. Years ago, I struggled with a grumpy gentleman at church who frequently lost his patience and scolded people. Eventually, dismayed at how often this happened, I brought it up to other church leaders. In response, I heard, "That's just how he is." I refused to accept that. Do we believe Christ can change people or not? Yes, we love people no matter what, but what does that love look like? Do we love people enough to believe they can be better, for their sake and ours?

However, accountability that works has to happen in the context of relationship. Consistency and familiarity provide essential ingredients. It's why people often listen to untrained family members more than trained nurses and doctors on health issues. Relationships often hold more power than expertise. No one invested more time and energy into relationships than Jesus.

Think back to the story of Zacchaeus. This tax collector consistently cheated his neighbors and found himself wealthy yet alone. When he hears of Jesus' visit to his town, he climbs a tree over the route just to get a glimpse of Jesus. Surprising to him, Jesus invites himself over to his house. Jesus initiates a relationship with him. The account in Luke 19 does not mention any words of accountability from Jesus. Yet, the sheer presence of Jesus moves Zacchaeus to ethical change. He promises to give half his possessions to the poor. To those he cheated, he commits to giving back four times the amount he stole. The relationship came first. The moral change came second. Jesus shows us this rhythm. Looking back, when I consider those who have held me accountable, many of them spent hours hanging out with me—worshipping together, going camping, talking sports, and eating together. Most of these relationships flowed in and out of church life.

After embracing the possibility of moral change and investing in relationships, we have to be willing to judge each other. At first glance, this appears unseemly as America's individualistic culture prides itself on not getting in each other's business. "Don't judge me" shows up often in our speech when we feel like someone has crossed the line into our space. On top of that, at face value, judging seems to conflict with the clear teaching of Jesus. In the Sermon on the Mount in Matthew 7:1, Jesus says, "Do not judge, or you too will be judged." There you have it, or so it seems.

Despite this seemingly nonjudgmental posture, this fact remains. We're a very judgmental society. A quick perusal of social media proves this. We freely lob accusations at each other, even people we know from afar. We judge each other as ignorant, biased, bigoted, and unchristian. Weekly, I'm amazed at our hostility towards judging alongside our willingness to engage in it early and often.

Not all of this is bad, though. After all, life demands that we make judgments. It's hard to get through the day without judgments. We have to judge the quickest route to work. We have to judge the best way to use our time. We have to judge the best way to have a difficult conversation with a friend. Life demands that we make judgments. So, consider the context of those times when we say, "Don't judge." We normally say it for one of two reasons. First, we use it as a deflective, defensive mechanism when we disagree. We don't like someone's opinion, so we call them "judgmental." We disagree with someone's take, so we call them "judgy." Second, we cry "Don't judge" when we find their judgments unfair. For example, when someone criticizes another without having all the information, we consider it unfair and therefore judgmental. When someone has no experience in a situation but pretends they do, we normally see that as unfair and therefore judgmental.

Reflecting on our usage, I realize some judgments never receive the "Stop judging" pushback. I say the following sensitively, but to prove a point. When we name perpetrators of genocide, racism, and abuse as wrong, no one ever responds with, "Why are you so judgmental?" Why? We agree on those judgments and find them to be fair. More than that, we judge those who fail to judge. Looking at those who don't speak out on genocide, racism, and abuse, we judge them as part of the problem even if not the direct perpetrators. Deep down, we know that some judgements prove necessary. We must make righteous judgments.

Amidst this reflection, Jesus' teaching offers a helpful perspective. Jesus believes we must make wise judgments, but we must avoid unfair judgments. Moreover, he points to a godly standard of judgment, which can't be deflected merely if you disagree. Let's return to the Sermon on the Mount, in Matthew 7:1–5.

> "Do not judge, or you too will be judged. For in the same way you judge others, you will be judged, and with the measure you use, it will be measured to you. Why do you look at the speck of sawdust in your brother's eye and pay no attention to the plank in your own eye? How can you say to your brother, 'Let me take the speck out of your eye,' when all the time there is a plank in your own eye? You hypocrite, first take the plank out of your own eye, and then you will see clearly to remove the speck from your brother's eye."

If we read the whole thing, we see that Jesus focuses his concern on unfair, hypocritical judgments. People judged others for doing the same things they did. They called out others for lying when they lied, for stealing when they stole. Jesus warns them that in the same way they judged, they would be judged. In verse 5, he teaches them to judge themselves first, so they can then judge each other properly. Stopping at verse 1 paints a picture of a "Mind your own business" Jesus. That caricature couldn't be further from the truth. Adding on to this, in John 7:24, we find, "Stop judging by mere appearances, but instead judge correctly." Jesus wants us to judge, but we must judge the right way with the right spirit.

Jesus shows us an order to our judgments that we must remember. We start with ourselves. Only after judging ourselves do we move outward. Paul elaborates on this further. In 1 Corinthians 5 he bemoans how the Corinthian church judged non-Christians in their town but gave each other a pass. He refers to an incestuous relationship inside the church, which they apparently took pride in tolerating. In verses 12, he says, "What business is it of mine to judge those outside the church? Are you not to judge those inside?"

Sadly, churches consistently violate this teaching. Part of the devastation of child abuse scandals in both Catholic and Protestant churches lay in this. Too many churches did not expel abusers from their positions even as they spoke out against the sexual sins of the world. They fixated on the world but gave each other a pass. This must not be so. When I talk to friends who have left church, this shows up as one of the main reasons.

When churches believe change is possible, invest in relationships, and practice fair, wise judgments, ethical transformation can happen. I've seen it. What does this look like? First off, it's not a program but a lifestyle. We must have a rhythm of being involved in the lives of our church family with grace and truth. Church leaders should consistently teach and preach on ethics. Tough topics should not be ignored. Consistently naming moral virtues from the Scriptures creates a necessary atmosphere. Alongside this, leaders must first hold other leaders to ethical standards. James 3:1 shows us that teachers will be judged more strictly. Why? Because hypocrisy hurts people. If a teacher and leader does not consistently live up to the ethics they teach, they should gracefully be removed for a season of repentance and healing.

Clearly, these ethical confrontations should happen face to face, which is easy to forget in our tech-saturated world. Jesus talks about loving confrontation in Matthew 18. Throughout, his focus is "Go to them." If we love people, we must ask if we love them enough to tell the truth. Face-to-face confrontation makes us pause. It's tough. It brings risk. What if they don't respond well? What if I lose the relationship? Yet, if we've done the work on the relationship, it often goes well.

Similar to the other unique aspects of church already mentioned, we've often neglected this ethical transformation. I think I know why. It's hard. It's uncomfortable. Sometimes, it leads to misunderstanding. Sometimes, people don't take it well and walk away. Yet, it's a necessary part of who we're meant to be. Without it, we're in danger. Faith profession without accountability leads to hypocrisy and denial. Perhaps the greatest sign of our brokenness lies in our inability to practice what we preach. People lose faith over it daily. The only way out of this is to seek ethical transformation through relationships focused on speaking the truth in love.

A few years back, I watched the series *Breaking Bad*. The show follows the path of a high school chemistry teacher, Walter White, into the world of organized crime, including making methamphetamine. Like others, I found the show compelling because of the nature of his descent into evil. At each crossroad, you can see why he makes the choices he makes. You can even empathize with him in spots. Each decision makes sense in a way even as he grows darker and darker. When I watched the show, one thing kept standing out—his ethical isolation. He didn't have friends with whom to express vulnerability and in whom to confide. He didn't have people in his life to tell him the cold hard truth when he needed to hear it. Without that, things got worse and worse and worse.

The other day, I found myself hanging out with a good friend, Spencer. We've known each other almost ten years and participate in church together. We found ourselves talking about a recurring pattern we see. We both have friends and acquaintances who possess so much talent, yet they have a debilitating weakness. Making it harder, they seem unaware of their weakness or at least unaware of its severity. Some have conversational quirks. Some lose their temper. Some can never get organized. Some always show up late. They don't realize how much they're missing because they've never gotten past these weaknesses.

In our conversation, Spencer and I wondered, "What if that happened to us? What if we had a debilitating weakness but no one ever told us?" So, I turned to him and said, "We should do that. We should tell each other our greatest weakness." The thought of that seemed freeing but also quite scary. We kept talking about it, but felt uneasy about actually doing it. Finally, he said, "Okay, we should do it. You start." I paused and said, "Are you serious? You really want me to?" "Yeah," he replied. "I'm ready." I calmly and gently looked him in the eye and said, "You struggle to follow through on things. Sometimes, you say you're gonna do something, but you don't always actually do it." It felt like too much as I said it. Would this work out? "Ouch," he replied, as if I'd hit him or something. It reminded me of trading punches with buddies back in middle school. "Ouch, that hurts, but you're right. I do have trouble following through." "Okay," I said, "It's your turn to tell me my weakness." I paused and prepared to take the hit. With complete clarity, he stated, "J.P., you have a tendency to make everything about you." "Ugh," I groaned. "Did you have to do that? Ouch. That hurts, but you're probably right. Ugh, I hate this." Ultimately, we laughed about it all, but I'll be honest. In the coming days, I noticed the many ways I overinterpret people and think their actions and words are about me. I do have a tendency to make things about me.

This realization makes me glad that I have people who love me enough to tell me the truth. They tell me when I have something on my face. They tell me, "You're better than that." Because they've done this over the years, I'm actually better. I'm by no means perfect, not even close. But God, through the Spirit, has used the church to make me more like Jesus. You can become more ethical. You can experience transformation. The church offers this.

The church offers all of this—open, weekly gatherings, intergenerational community, transnational identity, and ethical transformation. These unique attributes flow out of the nature of the church—the body of Jesus, the bride of Christ, and the social expression of the kingdom. This is the beauty of the church. When you experience this, when you embrace her, you immediately access a wealth of relationships and opportunity. You will begin to see why so many find that she's still worth it.

SECTION 3

Broken, Beautiful, and Worth it

15

Thick Culture

I HATE TRYING TO find a new dentist. It's one of the worst parts of moving. You have to find a new car guy. You have to find a new hairstylist or barber. You have to find new healthcare providers. When I got that first new job after college, I just didn't go to the dentist for a while. Eventually, I felt like I had to go. I asked a friend for a recommendation, and after making an appointment, I walked into an unfamiliar waiting room. People I'd never met before peered into my mouth. They had the audacity to comment on my brushing habits. They asked me to floss more. Who did these people think they were? I missed my dentist.

Growing up, I didn't always call my dentist "Dr. Speck." More often than not, I called him "Coach." He was my Little League baseball coach. His son, Travis, has always been one of my best friends. More than that, we all went to the same church. I saw Coach multiple times a week for years. Coach taught my Bible class. Coach hit me ground balls at practice. Coach served me Communion. Depending on the situation, Coach both encouraged and challenged me. Coach fixed my cavities and taught me how to brush. Coach showed up in multiple spheres of my life, which led to an overlap effect. Our relationship goes deep because of it.

When I was thirteen years old and in the seventh grade, the phone rang one winter morning. It was Coach asking to talk to me. "You playing baseball with us this year, Joe Paul?", asked Coach. "Absolutely," I said. "Okay. I'm signing up the team and wanted to double check. Get out there and practice some. Season will start before you know. Go run ten miles for me. Okay?" "Yes, Coach, I'll be ready."

We were underdogs that year. We'd lost some of our best players from the year before. At the same time, we added a bunch of kids I'd never met. As the season started, I realized one team was stacked. They boasted the entire all-star team from the year before, minus one. They didn't have Travis, who of course played with us on Coach's team. I remember thinking this seemed odd, even unfair. Quickly, I put it out of my mind. I loved playing baseball. I loved the smell of the grass and the chatter of the dugout. We had a good year, a little better than average. The stacked team of last year's all-stars went undefeated. In the postseason tournament, we won our first game. In the next game, we'd play the all-stars. I went into the game feeling intimidated, but Coach thought we could win. He told us that if we played our game, good things would happen. We scored a few runs early, and as the game wore on, we desperately tried to hold on to the lead. In the last inning, we were up one run. They had two outs and a man on second. One of their best hitters came to the plate. I paced back and forth at my shortstop position, kicking the dirt nervously. We just needed one more out. Travis did the same at his first base position. Coach encouraged us all, "One more out, guys. One more." After a few pitches, the batter hit a firm ground ball right at me. I fielded it cleanly and threw to first. As I let it go, my heart sank. It wasn't a great throw. It sailed on me, and I just knew it'd go over Travis's head and hit the fence. A tall kid, he stretched as high as he could. It felt like time stood still. I remember hearing the cheers of our crowd. Travis had caught the ball. Runner out. Game over. We beat them. I ran over to hug Travis. I remember my coach, dentist, Bible class teacher, and best friend's dad grabbing me. "You did it. I'm proud of you."

The next year went the exact opposite way. Travis and I joined a different league and had a different coach. Outmatched, we lost every single game. The games weren't even close. We lost by football scores: 24–7; 17–3. It was brutal. Years later, one significant moment stands out to me. Coach still went to our games and cheered from the stands. After another loss, probably the third or fourth one of the season, he drove us home. I'll never forget his speech. "Boys, you've got two choices. You can quit, or you can play as hard as you can knowing you'll likely get beat. You have two choices, but I'll tell you this. You're not quitters. That's not you. So, I hope you go out there and play hard with integrity even if you lose. If you do that, you'll prove what type of men you are." So, that's what we did. We got destroyed the entire year, yet I showed up to every game prepared to give it my all with the hope of victory. I struggled through that year, but honestly, I learned a lot more from losing than from winning. I owe much of that to Coach, as well as my parents and the other adults and coaches around that team.

I grew up in a thick culture. It provided overlapping webs of relationships that brought a type of social security to my life. Life stretches us. No matter how much we prepare, life will throw intense ups and downs at us. As we stretch, sometimes we feel we might break. Things might spin completely out of control. What stabilizes us in these times? Thick culture. My relationship with Coach is an example of that.

Scripture speaks of it in this way. Ecclesiastes 4:12 says, "A cord of three strands is not quickly broken." One strand doesn't stand much of a chance when the stretching comes. Two strands clearly prove stronger than one but still won't be strong enough for complicated challenges. However, the third strand forms a bond that is not easily severed. Coach wasn't just my coach. He wasn't just my dentist. He wasn't just a leader and teacher at my church. Coach was all three. Because he was all three, the relationship had a notable strength to it.

You might think of it in terms of spheres. Some divide life into the spheres of where you live, work, and play. The sphere of work includes school. I'd include a sphere of all types of third spaces—doctor's office, library, grocery store, gymnastics practice, etc. I'd add church as a sphere. When you know someone in one of those spheres, it has a certain level of familiarity and closeness to it. Normally though, if you know that person in more than one sphere, the intimacy deepens. I knew Coach in multiple spheres, so the relationship had a multilayered strength to it.

Relationships that only happen in one sphere usually represent thin culture. Someone you only know at the office. The nameless person who changes your oil. The neighbor across the street whom you wave at but struggle to come up with their name. These represent one-strand relationships. These types of relationships lead to thin culture.

About a decade ago, through my church, I entered into the world of homeless ministry and advocacy. I've learned so much by listening to my unhoused friends and neighbors. I've come to see the world in deeper, truer ways. Through an amazing organization called Room in the Inn, our church has hosted homeless men overnight.[1] Frequently, we'll stay up chatting, telling stories, and watching football. As I'm falling asleep on these nights, I ask myself, "How are these men different from me?" For the most part, they're not. We're all created in the image of God and possess a certain set

1. All royalties from the sale of this book go to support Room in the Inn.

of strengths and weaknesses. At least one thing is different, though. These guys have no one to call for a place to crash. Many have friends and even family members, but for various reasons, they don't stay with them. When I think about this, I start to add up the number of people I could call. The list gets close to one hundred. What is the difference? It's the difference between thin culture and thick culture. At some point, maybe through their choices or the choices of others, the cords of their life began to unravel. They began to cling to one strand, and it snapped. Clearly, those in need of housing need economic empowerment and material assistance. But it's more than that. They need relationships—the thicker the web, the better. Thin ropes snap. Thick ropes don't.

A few years back, I saw a tragic article about the Golden Gate Bridge.[2] Sadly, for years, it's been a destination for people who wanted to take their own life. The city has put up nets and taken steps to provide support for those with this very real struggle. When authorities went to the apartment of one deceased jumper, they found a heartbreaking message. "The guy was in his thirties, lived alone, pretty bare apartment. He'd written a note and left it on his bureau. It said, 'I'm going to walk to the bridge. If one person smiles at me on the way, I will not jump.'" Apparently, no one smiled at him. This story always stops me in my tracks. It's devastating. It's what thin culture looks like.

Modern American culture often promotes thinness. We live far away from work. We value privacy. Many of our relationships only offer one sphere. They're one strand relationships. Online relationships frequently harbor a thinness in disguise. We may feel close, but over time, lack of proximity and overlap reveals a thinness. Sadly, church relationships can even be this way if we're not careful. If our church life never intersects with our work, play, family, school, and neighborhood life, it's a one-strand relationship. Much of consumer Christianity unknowingly promotes thin culture.

My step grandfather knew that well. After working for most of his career as a college professor and administrator, he spent his retirement years promoting thick culture. For decades, he and my step-grandmother had been deeply involved in a local church. However, as it grew, it became harder and harder to connect everyone. So my grandfather committed to sitting down personally with every person who joined the church. Before and after worship, he stood by a kiosk in the foyer meeting people and helping them connect to all the ministries of the church. He greeted people by name.

2. Friend, "Jumpers."

He knew everyone. He connected people with a "You should meet so and so. They're interested in the same thing." Even nine years after his death, I continually meet people who light up and say, "I knew Norman. He always talked to me. He helped me meet people." They tell stories about how he got them connected. He knew modern American churches can be thin, but he wanted others to experience the thickness he had always known.

We see this thickness in the Bible. The early church promoted a multi-stranded cord. Notice the thickness of this culture in Acts 2, which I mentioned in chapter 7. They met together daily. The had all things in common. They shared their very lives together. Because they shared so much of their lives together, they wove a multilayered web of responsibility towards each other. Everything gets closer as distance shrinks. Thickness results.

I'll give you an example. Our friends Matt and Sarah live half a mile away. We're part of the same church. Our kids attended the same elementary school. When we ride bikes through the neighborhood, we're prone to stop unannounced to say hi. Matt has driven me to the airport. I've picked him up from work when they had car trouble. Their son has gotten my mail when we've gone out of town. The layers of our lives intersect in multiple spots. Matt is not just my neighbor. Matt wears all of these hats—elder in my church, father of one of my daughter's best friends, parent at our local school, and buddy to call for errands and household projects. Multilayered friendships provide a strength unmatched in other relationships.

Recently, Coach retired. For years, I've known this day would come. In recent years, I've driven my daughters to the other side of town so Coach could be their dentist too. But those days are now over. I had to find another dentist. Several friends gave me recommendations, but I had pretty high expectations. I'd grown accustomed to my dentist being my mentor, confidant, and friend. I couldn't imagine going to a stranger. I wanted a relationship, not just a teeth-cleaning. At my kid's soccer practice one night, I saw one of the other parents, Sam. I'd heard he worked as a dentist, so I walked over to ask if he might have space for more patients. Sam readily agreed, but I had a question to ask him. "I'm accustomed to being really close to my dentist. I've had the same dentist most of my life—a family friend, one of the great mentors of my life. You got time for that?" He laughed and told me he'd do his best. So far, so good.

I think back to my days in Little League baseball. I think of the years Coach Speck led our team. Every time I think about beating that all-star team, a smile comes to my face. Years later, I learned something that makes that memory even sweeter. My friend Travis told me this story. Remember, years before, Coach called me one late winter morning to ask me if I planned to play that year. Remember that Travis was the only kid from the previous year's all-star team not on the new loaded team. What was that all about? As it turns out, they recruited Travis for their team. They wanted Coach to coach with them. As they discussed it, he simply asked, "Well, we go way back with Joe Paul and want him on our team. Is there a spot for him?" The voice on the other end said no. "Well," Coach said, "then we wouldn't be able to join your team. We're with Joe Paul."

Looking back, I wonder why my life has turned out the way it has. I have had my fair share of disappointments, yet I've blessings I didn't deserve. Near the top of that list, I have experienced a close-knit church community that possessed all four of the unique qualities mentioned in the previous chapters. Church has been worth it because it has given me a thick culture, and my life has been far richer because of it. When we have a strong support system of multilayered relationships, we experience a treasure many miss out on. The value of all these relationships adds up. We come to possess social capital, a wealth of relationships. Thick culture leads to social capital, and I'll explore that in the next chapter.

16

Social Capital

I LIKE DRINKING COKE out of glass bottles. It feels high class. As a kid, when we got the treat of drinking Coke, it came in plastic two-liter bottles. We didn't get to order Coke at restaurants. Every now and then, we might get a canned soda. But on rare occasions, we got to drink out of glass bottles. I loved it. For one, it tasted better than drinking out of plastic or aluminum. On top of that, since it was a special treat, it had the air of wealth. When I drank Coke out of glass bottles, I felt rich.

My experiences with glass-bottled Coke mostly came from trips down to Bridgeport, Alabama. My dad grew up there, and we made the two-hour pilgrimage down there once or twice a year. Most every time, we went to the Melton's house, an elderly family that apparently knew Dad as he grew up. We weren't blood related, but they treated my dad like a son in many ways. Therefore, they felt like pseudo-grandparents to me. Mr. Melton always ushered me and my brother out into the garage. In an old fridge, he showed us a seemingly endless supply of glass-bottled Cokes. My older brother and I didn't have to share. We each got our own. I always felt spoiled by this gesture. I'd sit down at their table awash in their hospitality. I'd hold up the glass bottle to watch it refract a glimpse of sunlight. Then, I'd tip it back and enjoy the classic taste of Coke. I felt rich.

My father grew up in abject poverty in rural Alabama in the 1950s and 1960s. His father, William, the son of an Irish immigrant, never graduated from high school. My grandfather spent most of his working career as a carpenter. Throughout his life, he struggled with both alcohol and gambling addiction. The Conways lived in simple rental properties on the poor side of town. Dad remembers not having what other kids had. Particularly, he recounts one Christmas when he got a shiny new bike. A few weeks later, the bike got repossessed as my grandfather couldn't make the payments on it. This was my dad's life, until it all changed.

Around the age of sixteen, buddies from school kept inviting him to church with them. The Conways didn't attend church, but this group of friends kept asking him. One week, some adults had planned a youth night on a Sunday evening at the church building. They'd be playing games and eating snacks. When they asked him this time, he turned to another friend and said, "I'll go if you go." That night changed his life. Dad encountered a group of people who smiled when they saw him and welcomed him into their lives. Quickly, church participation became the rhythm of his life. His mother, Alberta, began to join him at worship. At seventeen, he asked to be baptized. Dad surrendered his life to Christ, and the church became his family.

Around this time, one of the church elders asked my dad, "What are you going to do after high school?" You see, Dad made good grades and even graduated as the valedictorian of his senior class. He had a reputation as a responsible kid. So this gentleman asked him about his future plans. Dad hadn't thought too much about it. He assumed he'd continue his job as a teller at the local bank. Due to his social location of poverty, he hadn't entertained too many options. He might chip away at a degree at the local community college eventually. "Well," said the older gentleman, "if you'd like to go to college, I'll pay for you to go." Dad couldn't believe his ears. He'd never met someone who could say stuff like that. He'd never encountered such wealth. After working for a year after high school to get his parents in a better situation, this guy sent Dad to David Lipscomb College (now Lipscomb University). The rest is history. Dad graduated with a math degree, met and married my mom, and served in public education for thirty-five years.

Growing up, I had this common occurrence. I'd walk through the kitchen at night around bedtime. Often, Dad would be standing in the kitchen eating milk and crackers. This always made me curious. He'd crush saltine crackers into a big cup (normally a souvenir-type cup from a sporting event) and pour milk over it. "Dad, why are you eating that?" It never looked appetizing to me. He never had much of answer. He'd just smile and say, "It reminds me of when I was poor." Because Dad got an education and a solid job as a schoolteacher, I didn't grow up poor. You would likely consider us middle class, yet Dad would often tell us we were rich. Compared to where he'd come from, we were. I remember asking him once, "Dad, when did you first feel like you were rich?" I assumed the answer would be "When I bought my first car" or "When I bought my first house." Nope. He answered, "The first time I ate in the college cafeteria, I knew I was rich."

This is social capital. Often, we think of capital in a material way—bank accounts, houses, cars, etc. That is of course true. Much of capital is material, but there exists other forms of capital. A much-neglected form of capital, especially in individualistic societies, takes shape in the form of social capital. Through your network of social relationships, you derive resources. Think of it this way. When your car breaks down, you know people who can help you get home. When you don't know what's wrong with it, you know people who understand cars or who know a good mechanic. While your car is getting worked on, you know people who can give you a ride to work or help you get your kids home from school. If you don't have enough money to fix the car, you know people who can loan you money at no interest. This is social capital.

Church exists as one of the richest forms of social capital in our society. For example, if you come to my church, I can offer you a wealth of connections. I can connect you with computer experts who can fix your computer for you and show you how to set parental controls in a way that actually work. I can connect you with nurses, doctors, and researchers who can explain what your physician quickly told you at your last rushed appointment. They can explain the diagnosis your family member recently received. They can help you navigate the healthcare system. I can connect you with social workers who can help you or someone you know navigate housing support as well as WIC and SNAP benefits. I can connect you with lawyers who can offer wise counsel as well as direct you towards a suitable attorney. I can connect you with skilled laborers in plumbing, electrical work, basic home remodeling, tree removal, and pest control who will help you with your own projects or tell you how much you should really be paying for a service. I can connect you with teachers who can help you understand the education system, college application process, and even help tutor your child. I can hook you up with all of this from my little church of 150 people. I can't give you much money, but I can make you rich. I can share my social capital.

A friend of mine, Thomas, told me this story years ago. He grew up in church, but for a variety of reasons he had ceased his involvement. Honestly, he harbored a lot of frustration towards the church—hypocrisy, racism, arrogance, you name it. One day, he ran into a childhood friend who challenged him to get back into a local congregation. As he tells the story, he told himself, "I'm gonna pick a big church in a rich part of town. I'm gonna walk in, and they're all gonna ignore me. They're gonna be everything I thought they were. Then, I'm gonna walk out one last time." But that's not what happened. When Thomas walked into this big, rich church in the suburbs, they welcomed him. They befriended him. More than that, over time, they connected him with a variety of resources. He told me he'd never had more connections and opportunities in his entire life. Because of his relationships among his new church, his social capital surged. It completely changed his life.

Church offers a wealth of social capital. It has been this way from the very beginning. In the New Testament, we see the sharing of material capital early and often. A scripture like Acts 2:45 describes it: "they sold property and possessions to give to anyone who had need." Acts 4:34 even says, "there were no needy persons among them." As they shared food, housing, and money, we see their generosity. Notice that it's not a blind transaction void of relationship. This capital has a social component. One of my favorite examples of this shows up in a scripture easy to miss. At the end of Paul's letter to the church in Rome, he offers a series of personal greetings to those in Rome but also from those with him in Corinth. Specifically, notice verse 23. "Gaius, whose hospitality I and the whole church here enjoy, sends you his greetings. Erastus, who is the city's director of public works, and our brother Quartus send you their greetings." At this point, the church consisted of a tiny minority. Yet, they had already attracted some movers and shakers. You see that the public works director of Corinth, Erastus, had become a disciple of Jesus. No doubt, he had sway in the city. He had influence and connections. You see another brother in the greeting, Quartus. His name simply means "Fourth." Who names their kid Fourth? It's not a personal name. It has no warmth. Most likely, a master gave this name to a slave. Most scholars believe that Quartus was a slave or former slave. Obviously, he would have held a low position in society with few connections or influence. But the church proves different than society. As part of the church, Quartus held many connections. He was buddies with Erastus, the public works director, and knew Paul well. The church represented perhaps the only path in society of that time for someone to expand their social capital to this degree.

The richness of the church community has been one of the great joys of my life. It's so seeped into my life that I see it everywhere. About seven years ago, we moved houses. It was a short move, just a mile from our old house. Beth asked me if I wanted to hire movers. "Why would I hire movers?" I asked. "We have a church. Why would I need movers?" Of course, my buddies may get to the point when they wish I'd hire a mover. But this is how I think of the church. I turn to her first. It's only when she can't help that I turn elsewhere. The church is my first call.

Helping someone move is a small thing, but I regularly see enormous, life-changing exchanges of capital similar to my father's story. Years ago, I went to a church with Rick and Jessica. While their son was in middle school, he became friends with another young man. This boy came from a challenging family context. For multiple reasons, his family did not provide him with all that he needed for success. Over time, Rick and Jessica saw this. Slowly at first, they stepped in. They became friends with the young man's family. They didn't want to be a threat but a resource. Over time, their relationship grew. They brought him to church with them, and he spent the night frequently at their home in a room set up just for him. They helped him navigate academics, finances, and relationships. As college neared, they brainstormed possibilities and shared advice. Eventually, the young man graduated college and got a good job. On the day of his wedding, Rick and Jessica sat near the front with the family, because they were family to him.

Early on in my ministry, Beth and I provided similar capital to many teenagers. One young man, Damian, spent the night at our house once a week. Regularly, we helped him with his homework. Another young man, Michael, had a key to our house. I remember the day I helped Jacky, a high school senior, fill out her FAFSA forms. Even now, we get calls late at night. "We have to run to the hospital. Can you come over and watch our kids?" We get last-minute texts. "Things blew up at work. Can you pick my kids up from school?"

Just the other day, an elderly woman at our church expressed the need for a new couch. When a person heard that, they quickly put the need out on a church email. Within thirty minutes, someone responded that they had a quality couch they no longer needed. By the end of the day, another person volunteered their truck and delivered it. Not every situation may seem life changing, yet, consistently applied, this type of connectivity leads to great social wealth.

Social capital goes beyond what financial capital provides. You can't put a price tag on it. This relational affluence shows up in desperate emergencies. Over a thirty-six-hour window on May 1–2, 2010, the city of Nashville received upwards of fourteen inches of rain. Meteorologists considered it the type of event that only comes every five hundred years. Around town, we simply refer to it as "the flood." At the time, I lived on a hill. If you'd asked me if I feared a flood, I would have laughed. But as the rain kept coming, I noticed water pooling up all around my house. I began to realize that my house sat just a tad lower than other houses on my street. Eventually, water surrounded my house and began to come into my bonus room (an old converted garage). I didn't know what to do. I didn't have a pump. I didn't have sandbags. In desperation, I grabbed a couple of buckets and started carrying water from the flooding room through the house and out to a side of the house where water hadn't come in yet. Gradually, neighbors and a few family members started coming over. A bucket line quickly ensued, but as hard as we worked, we couldn't keep up.

My phone kept ringing. It was my friend, Greg, who went to church with me. From others, he'd heard I had water coming into the house. I knew roads were shut down because of the flooding. From the news, I knew cars had gotten stuck. People had even died. Greg lived about a thirty-minute drive from my house. I didn't want him to risk his safety to come to me, so I just ignored my ringing phone. Still, the water kept rising. I got more and more nervous as the water inched up the edge of the main floor of the house. We kept the bucket line going. It was like nothing I'd ever experienced. Then, I looked up and saw Greg. He stood in my front yard holding a pump, the very thing I needed. Because of the pump, as well as my brother-in-law unclogging my drainage ditch, the water began to abate. When I didn't answer the phone, Greg just got in his car and drove anyway. I don't know how much money in damage I saved because of Greg's generosity. I know this, though. Because of him, I felt rich. I can't put a price tag on what he did that day.

The church provides four unique qualities which lead to thick culture. In turn, thick culture leads to social capital. She gives us relational support that makes us socially wealthy, despite our material circumstances. In a world that too often continues to struggle with the plight of poverty, I hear lots of worthwhile solutions. Let me add one more—the social capital of the church.

I don't drink Coke often, but when I do, I like to drink it out of a glass bottle. I like to go out back and sit on my porch swing. When I do, I hold up the glass bottle to see the sunlight refract through the glass. I think to myself, "I'm a rich man", because I am. When I drink a glass-bottled Coke, I almost always think of Mr. Melton ushering me and my brother out to the garage for a Coke. He wasn't my grandfather, but in those moments he treated me like family. I often wondered why he and my dad felt such a close connection. Earlier, I mentioned that a family at Dad's church had paid his way to college. That family was the Meltons. My dad was dirt poor, but when he met Jesus, he encountered Jesus' family. In doing so, Dad became rich—physically, spiritually, and emotionally. Mr. Melton sent my dad to college, where he got an education, met my mom, and changed the trajectory of my life. Because of that, we went down every year to say thank you to the Meltons. That relationship, found and formed within church, made us rich.

When I calculate my wealth, I don't look at my bank account. I don't check my retirement savings or the value of my house. I look at my church. She's worth a lot. I don't have the most money in the world, but I can't imagine being any more rich.

17

The Common Good

I LIVE IN A religious city. Signs of religion cover the landscape of Nashville. In the spring of 1978, my mother gave birth to me at what was then called Baptist Hospital. One of the main other hospitals in town bore the name Saint Thomas Hospital. I grew up with the expectation that most hospitals had religious names. I never thought much about it. Years later, over a six-year span, my wife gave birth to all three of our children in the same hospital, now absorbed into the Saint Thomas system. As I drive through my hometown, I see numerous colleges and universities with Christian origins—Vanderbilt, Belmont, Fisk, Lipscomb, Trevecca, Aquinas, Welch, and American Baptist. In the raising of our three daughters, we have been reminded that most preschools and youth sports leagues in our city find their homes in and around local churches. When it comes to those churches, our city boasts about a thousand congregations along with around a thousand nonprofit organizations, most of which have religious roots or affiliation. I have spent thirty-two of my forty-two years in and around this city, and I cannot imagine it without the Christian church. Without faith, Nashville would not be the same. More than just my city, I believe the entire world is better because of Christianity.

Not everyone believes that, of course. I realized this in the weeks and months after 9/11 as well as the years of war in its aftermath. If religion produces such historic hostility, many openly wondered if the world would be better off without it. Honestly, as I have already confessed, it's fairly easy to find evidence of religion's, even Christianity's, contribution to the world's evil. We could cite the Crusades, the Inquisition, and justifications for slavery, to name a few. In contemporary American culture, many point to the religious undertone of the culture wars as further evidence for their belief that religion does more harm than good. Still, when the math is over, when all the additions and subtractions of the church have been calculated, I think the sum of the good will outweigh the bad. Our world is better with the church than without her. The church uniquely contributes to human flourishing and promotes the common good.

In fact, this has always been one of the primary purposes of the church—to bless the world. Whether it's God's promise to bless all peoples through Abraham's seed or Jesus' affirmation of the centrality of loving neighbor, God has always sought this rhythm. God transforms individuals who make up communities. These transformed communities transform the world. The church has always existed for the sake of the world. When she's forgotten that, well, those times represent the brokenness. But when she's remembered her calling, it's truly been something to witness.

For me, the most moving instructions on blessing the city come from Jeremiah 29, another story of exile. In the sixth century B.C., a foreign enemy, Babylon, captured the Hebrews and took them far from home. Like any conquered people, two instincts surfaced, resentment and assimilation. Some longed for Babylon's destruction. Some wanted to become Babylonians. In contrast to these two options, Jeremiah charts a third option—seek the good of Babylon while remaining who you are.

Jeremiah told them to build houses, plant gardens, and get married. The prophet encouraged them to settle down and make a life for themselves. They were to seek the welfare of the city, the common good. If Babylon prospered, they would prosper. Their fortunes were linked. Exile should not lead to resentment or assimilation. Rather, they should seek the good of their new neighbors. In the same chapter, Jeremiah proclaimed that their exile would only last seventy years. The prophet offered these words of encouragement in verse 11: "For I know the plans I have for you, plans to prosper you and not harm you, plans to give you hope and a future." Exile was temporary. God had not forgotten his people. Their future remained bright. Because they had a promised future, they should live fully in the present without resorting to resentment or assimilation.

Likewise, Christians cling to the hope of the future new heaven and new earth. This world, in its present broken form, is passing away. God will redeem and renew this good creation. However, this truth does not cause us to withdrawal, but to invest. Christians must seek the good of the city. The church works for the common good.

When the church has forgotten these words of Jeremiah, we have seen the great acts of brokenness. Abuse, hatred, and oppression come when Christians assimilate to the desires of selfishness and power. These evils fester and grow when the church has withdrawn into the cliché of the frozen chosen. However, when the church seeks the welfare of the city, you see hospitals, universities, and nonprofit organizations making the world better for everyone. To me, this is beautiful.

As I write this chapter, my family shelters at home as part of a citywide "safer at home" quarantine for the COVID-19 virus. Likely, you have experienced a similar quarantine as part of our united efforts to confront the pandemic. As this tragedy has grown and spread, I have seen churches join the front lines of the fight, whether that be sewing masks, supplying food, or checking on elderly neighbors. It has been quite a year in Nashville as a tornado ripped through our community just a week or so before the virus arrived. In the days after the storm, volunteers flooded into the community, many of them Christians working individually or through church groups and ministries. On some days, the heavy response of the volunteers actually made it hard to find work to do. Several told me they showed up on work sites only to leave after a few minutes because the crowds had already gotten the work done. I'm thankful for these friends and neighbors. Throughout Christian history, the church has uniquely shown up, time and time again, to love its cities.

When thinking of this history, I often go back to the work of historian Gary Ferngren. His book *Medicine and Healthcare in Early Christianity* details how the early church shaped our world's views on the sick and how to care for them. While healthcare, medicine, and the physician profession existed before Christianity, the notion of the hospital came from disciples of Jesus.[1] Unbelievably, in the ancient world, the sick often received blame for their condition. Moreover, Ferngren says, "Human worth was not regarded in the classical world as intrinsic."[2] However, Christians lived by a different conviction and embraced all humans as image-bearers of a holy God. This radically changed how they lived in general, but specifically how they practiced healthcare. Based on the example of Jesus, Christians demonstrated an "emphasis on caring more than curing," walking alongside the sick regardless of outcome.[3] This countercultural way of approaching the sick and

---

1. Ferngren, *Medicine and Healthcare*, 83.

2. Ferngren, *Medicine and Healthcare*, 95.

3. Ferngren, *Medicine and Healthcare*, 145.

marginalized contributed to the growth of the church. One such example comes from the Plague of Cyprian in the mid-third century. While the wealthy elite ran for the hills, many Christians got down in the trenches and helped each other and their neighbors. Because of this, Christians survived the plague at a higher rate. In addition, the care and solidarity expressed for the sick persuaded many of the survivors to embrace the Christian faith. When the church is for the common good, everyone prospers.

We need healthy churches, for they provide essential services for their communities. In fact, many sociologists and economists have sought to calculate the value of churches. Researchers call this the "halo effect." A study associated with the University of Pennsylvania's School of Social Policy and Practice estimates that "the average urban historic sacred place generates over 1.7 million in economic impact daily."[4] This same study found that "87% of the beneficiaries of the community programs and events housed in sacred places are not members of the religious congregation." The Halo Project out of Canada found that for every dollar a religious congregation spends on its services, a city gets $4.77 worth of common-good services.[5] Much of this comes from on-site programs that churches offer, including after-school programs and support classes. A significant part of this comes from volunteer hours generated by the community. A potentially ignored element of this though comes from impacts on the individual. Sociologists add a calculated benefit for "a church's impact on areas like suicide prevention, employment assistance, crime prevention, helping end substance abuse, counseling, education, immigration assimilation, and so on."[6] Every time a church intervenes to take care of the sick, keep someone from turning back to crime, or helping someone find freedom from addiction, it takes a strain off the social system. Churches reduce the volume of those who need hospitals, end up in prison, or turn to social services. In doing so, churches help the local economy and support the social fabric.

In my city, if all churches ceased to exit, everyone would suffer. We would all be worse off. While I could point to many examples, I'll focus on two, the homeless crisis and local public schools. In Nashville, many estimate that we have around 20,000 who lack consistent, secure housing. For decades churches have been on the front lines. In 1953, the California preacher Charles Fuller led a revival at the historic Ryman Auditorium, the

4. Partners for Sacred Spaces, "Economic Halo Effect."
5. Halo Project, "Halo Calculator."
6. Sunde, "Halo Effect."

"Mother Church of Country Music." During his trip, he encountered many on the streets without housing. When he returned to California, he returned his honorarium, asking that it be used to help those he encountered. This triggered the opening of the Nashville Rescue Mission, which houses up to 500 men year round at its downtown location as well as providing housing for women and children at its North Nashville location.

Another essential voice in this work comes from Room in the Inn, which I mentioned in chapter 15. In 1985, Father Charles Strobel invited the homeless encamped in his church's parking lot to take shelter inside. Within a year, four other churches joined in the effort to shelter unhoused individuals in their facilities. Today, nearly 200 congregations of a wide array of traditions shelter between 150 and 300 men and women every night from November 1 to March 31. Specifically, my congregation hosts 6 men every Sunday night during the Room in the Inn season. Sharing a meal with these guests, alongside my children, has expanded my world and altered my perceptions.

For homeless families, we have Safe Haven Family Shelter. It began at Saint Patrick Church in South Nashville, and now has its own beautiful facility. When it comes to placing people in housing and reaching out to those who fall through the cracks of traditional shelter options, we look to Open Table Nashville. All of these groups were started by churches or maintain consistent engagement in and through churches. To be clear, government plays a role in working to alleviate the housing crisis. I am grateful for good governance. Yet any government official in Nashville would tell you that churches form the front lines in fighting for these image-bearers.

Second, churches serve on the front lines in supporting kids' education. Metro Nashville Public Schools has 86,000 students and over 167 schools. United4Hope works to pair congregations with local schools. They train church volunteers on how to work appropriately with schools as well as secure background checks. Around a third of Nashville schools now have a church partner through United4Hope. Volunteers provide tutoring, reading, and mentoring services. In addition, they provide teacher encouragement and resources for parents. Some schools have experienced dramatic turn-arounds in reading proficiency because of church volunteer efforts. My congregation works with an elementary school down the street from our church building, and my weekly reading sessions with my student prove a weekly highlight. At my kids' elementary school, down the street from my house, I'm constantly reminded of the role of local churches. The neighborhood Baptist and Methodist churches both provide after-school programs. I think of another Baptist church a couple of miles from my home. They allow students from the adjacent high school to use their parking lot. Over eight years, all three of our daughters attended their preschool at various times. We've been frequent participants in their youth basketball league as well. We've never attended a worship service with them, yet they've forever shaped our lives as well as the lives of the children and families of our neighborhood.

The communal benefits from churches translate to individual transformation. Studies show that religious practitioners live longer than the average American. A study by Laura Wallace, with Ohio State University, found the life extension to be about four years.[7] The Duke Center for Spirituality, Theology, and Health cites an increase of eight years as well as reduced rates of depression, anxiety, and loneliness.[8] MIT economist Jonathan Gruber found that living densely among those with similar religious beliefs leads to an increased level of religious participation, "as well to better outcomes according to several key economic indicators: higher levels of education and income, lower levels of welfare receipt and disability, higher levels of marriage, and lower levels of divorce."[9] Participating in a healthy church makes you healthier, and in turn it makes your neighborhood healthier.

Jesus did not create the church to exist for herself, but for the world. Just as Jesus sacrificed his body on the cross, he expects his body, the church, to sacrifice herself for the good of others. The church, when she lives up to her calling through the power of the Spirit, contributes to human flourishing and promotes the common good. She makes our cities better. Because of that, my city knows she's worth it.

7. "One Thing You'll Find."
8. Center for Spirituality, Theology, and Health, "Welcome."
9. Gruber, "Religious Market Structure."

18

An Opportunity to Grow

ABOUT A DOZEN YEARS ago, I witnessed committed Christians have a knock-down, drag-out argument over Sonic tater tots. This bizarre scenario occurred at our annual summer camp. We had an amazing week together with adults and college students volunteering as counselors and staff for 175 kids and teenagers. We swam in a huge pool which even included a twisty slide. We shot fireworks. We played competitive games like soccer and softball, as well as silly games like chocolate sundae tug-of-war. We sang songs and laughed a ton. But on the last day, things kind of fell apart. The camp director had a rule that no one should leave the property unless necessary. To no one's surprise, the camp food got old after a few days, and some counselors wanted to make a fifteen-minute run over to Sonic. On this last night, some weary counselors exited the mess hall to find a group of their fellow counselors rolling back into camp with bags full of burgers and tater tots with slushies and sodas in their hands. They had broken the rule. One thing led to another, and I walked out to find this previously pious group of Christian mentors intensely arguing and making various accusations at one another. Motives were impugned on both sides. Fingers were pointed. Disparaging comments about previous actions came out. Sadly, some of the campers walked out to see this. The satisfaction of a week of warm memories and spiritual renewal disappeared in an instant. It was quite ugly and discouraging.

Why is church so hard? Tempers flare. Relationships wither. Scandals pile up. Conflict stirs over the most benign issues. Needed changes sometimes take years. Countless times, I've sat with hurting people struggling to be a part of the local church. Why is church so hard? I've been asked that more than once. It's a good question, and I've wrestled with it a long time. Here's how I process it.

Church is hard because growth is hard. Think of it this way. Why is training for a marathon hard work? In my mid-twenties, I saw a flyer advertising a marathon in my city. Since I'd always wanted to run a marathon, I saw this as an opportunity. Whereas I previously ran three to four miles about three days a week, this new goal called for me to extend those distances in preparation for a 26.2-mile race. My body ached. My mind grew bored during these runs over an hour in length. I didn't always enjoy the training, but I pressed on to the goal. My runs now extended up to twelve, fourteen, sixteen, eighteen, and ultimately twenty miles. This took so much more time. Some days, I didn't want to get out of bed. My feet were so sore. My knees wobbled. At this point, I wondered if this was truly an opportunity or a disaster. Still, as I trained, I grew stronger and stronger. Eventually, race day came, and because of my preparation, I finished my first marathon. I grew so much from that experience, and I'll never forget the joy of crossing the finish line. You can't just get out of bed one day and run a marathon. You have to train. Why is the training so hard? Because growth hurts.

The church proves similar. What is the mission of the church? If the church exists as the body of Christ, then the goal centers on becoming one with Jesus. The mission revolves around growing like Jesus to expand his kingdom in this world. In Colossians 1:15, Paul says Jesus is the "image of the invisible God." Later, in Colossians 3:10, he discusses how disciples have "put on the new self which is being renewed in knowledge in the image of its Creator." Jesus is the image of God. As the Spirit does its work on us, we become formed into that image. We become more and more like Jesus.

In and of myself, I'm not much like Jesus. The thought of becoming like him makes a marathon sound easy. What would it take to become like him? What means does God use for this training? Church exists as part of our training for Christlikeness. Participating in church is like working out. Like any training, it's hard work. This perspective shift can really shape our expectations.

I'm reminded of a similar refrain, this time in the realm of marriage. Some time ago, Gary Thomas wrote a bestseller on marriage entitled *Sacred Marriage: What If God Designed Marriage to Make Us Holy More Than to*

Make us Happy?[1] I like that idea not only because I believe it to be true, but because of the perspective change. If one approaches marriage as a means towards the end goal of happiness, then one will inevitably question the marriage through times of unhappiness. That's an unrealistic goal for marriage, though. Marriage proves so hard because the proximity of the relationships leaves little space to hide our weakness. I can hide my flaws around others, but it's almost impossible to hide my selfishness and pride from my wife. My marriage reveals my sin. In those moments, it's tempting to be unhappy. But in reality, that's a sign that marriage has done its job. In those moments, marriage gives me an opportunity to grow and be a better person.

Leveraging Thomas's phrasing, think of it this way. What if God designed church to make us like Jesus more than to make us happy? If this is true, and I think it is, then it radically adjusts our expectations. Why is church hard? Because growing into the image of Jesus is hard. Because growing into the image of Jesus is good and beautiful. If my church life brings challenges, I could see the problem as the church. Or, I could see those challenges as an opportunity to grow, mature, and become like Jesus. When church is hard, it's not that it's failed. If church is hard, it's done its job.

Years ago, when I served as a youth minister, a disagreement among some teens cast a cloud over our whole group. Katie and Jessie had been best friends for over a year. Katie began to date Curt, and the three of them would often hang out. After a few months of dating, they broke up, and very quickly Curt and Jessie began dating. Not surprisingly, this caused some hurt feelings between the two girls. Gossip reigned. In a matter of days, people took sides and declared allegiances. We had Team Katie and Team Jessie. This undercurrent lasted for weeks even as we all worshipped together.

As we neared our annual fall retreat, I grew tired of the division and wondered how we could help each other become more like Jesus. I never told any of them the reason, but we made *shalom*, or peace, the theme of the weekend. We read Jesus' teaching on peace, reconciliation, and conflict management. We studied how Jesus handled relationships, and we had breakout groups to make application to our lives. On the last night, we designed a series of self-guided spiritual reflections which took people on a journey from the basement of the lodge to the top floor. While on the main floor, they faced this challenge. As they read the instructions in their notebook, they discovered they had to be at peace, or at least make an effort towards peace, with every single person on the retreat before they could

---

1. Thomas, *Sacred Marriage.*

move up to the top floor. Many students and adults apologized for various things they'd said or done in recent months. Eventually, we all moved up to the top floor—everyone, that is, except Katie and Jessie. To their credit, they took the challenge to become more like Jesus. They did the hard work of apologizing to each other. It took a while. I still remember the feeling I had when they entered the top floor. Peace reigned. They put aside division and did the hard work, led by the Spirit, of growing like Jesus. This is what the church is meant to do.

Church is not an end in itself. The goal is not to get people in church. The goal is not to attend church. The goal is formation into the image of Jesus. Church participation exists as a growth opportunity. When the apostle Paul talked about this, he used a specifically descriptive and painful analogy. In Galatians 4:19, we read, "My dear children, for whom I am again in the pains of childbirth until Christ is formed in you." When we walk with others as they become formed into Christ, we'll experience pain. It's unpleasant and difficult at times. For training to do its job, it must be challenging. Church participation is training for becoming like Jesus. To be clear, Paul does not seem deterred by this pain. Throughout his writings and life, he shows that hardship plays a key role in our development. Notice the progression he describes in Romans 5:3. "We also glory in our sufferings, because we know that suffering produces perseverance; perseverance, character; and character, hope."

I've experienced this in church life. I say this tongue in cheek, but people are the worst. I am the worst, right? When we consistently spend time together as church, we'll inevitably hurt one another. Many times, I've hurt others. Many times, others have hurt me. More than that, through my interaction with the church, I've realized the ways I fall short of Jesus' example. If we persevere through the challenge and come out on the other side, we can experience growth and hope. On top of that, if we learn to see the hardship of church life as an opportunity to grow in character, it changes our perspective. It shapes our expectations. We're not here to consume a religious experience. We're working out together.

Here's the problem, though. Because we have the wrong expectation of church, we see the challenge of church life as something to avoid. When we leave the work out, we miss the opportunity for growth. My sophomore year of high school, I joined the track team. My coach assigned me to the distance group, and I began running the mile and two-mile. I had much to learn about running, especially the idea of pace. Early in a race, I'd feel the urge to quit. My body couldn't keep the pace. Coach, along with wiser teammates, would call, "Keep going. You'll get your second wind." I'd heard people say that before, but I never knew what it was. I found it to be true. Even now, when I'm out running, I'll feel the urge to quit. More often than not, though, if I keep going, eventually I get that second wind. My body adjusts. I feel stronger. Trusting that the second wind would come, that was a major part of my growth as a runner.

Formation into the image of Christ reminds me of this. Church involvement will make us tougher, deeper disciples as long as we don't walk away. I'll choose one potential growth area as an example—conflict management. In Matthew 18, Jesus gives specific instruction on how to handle conflict. If someone wrongs you, go directly to them. The principle centers on this. Pursue direct face-to-face communication and resist gossip. Only involve more people if it doesn't go well.

When someone wrongs me, my impulse is to lash out at them or talk poorly about them to others. Jesus takes both of these options off the table. The options he lays out demonstrate wisdom but seem overwhelming to most of us. Patient, gentle, and direct communication is really hard. Yet, that's the option Jesus gives. Just the other day, a friend in my church confronted me. She harbored frustration over how I communicated something. She calmly explained how it came across to her. Honestly, my first instinct centered on defensiveness, but I tried to calm that impulse. I listened and tried to understand her perspective. I affirmed her concerns and explained what had led to my communication and the intentions surrounding it. I apologized. Within five minutes, we understood one another. No gossip. No drama. Because of the calm way she approached it, resolution came easily. This is what maturity looks like, and we don't develop it overnight. We practice it consistently. Church provides an avenue for practice.

Along these lines, I think of another example—forgiveness. In Matthew 6:14–15, Jesus says, "For if you forgive other people when they sin against you, your heavenly Father will also forgive you. But if you do not forgive others their sins, your Father will not forgive your sins." Forgiving someone might be the hardest of all Christian practices. To be clear, we should not force or pressure people to forgive. It takes time, but once again, the church provides ample opportunity to practice. At my church growing up, one of our members fell into immoral and illegal behavior. It shocked all of us. People lost sleep over it. Out on bail and awaiting his trial, he got permission from the other leaders to attend one of our evening services. At the end of the service, he approached the front of the sanctuary to talk to the minister. He wanted to express regret and remorse. He wanted to ask forgiveness of the entire church. It all felt very uncomfortable. The minister led a prayer on his behalf, and the service concluded. Some people walked down front to greet him face to face. Some did not. Following my parents' example, I walked to the front. I didn't want to forgive him, but I did. I gave him a hug and told him I loved him. Certainly, this did not take away the consequences of his actions. Honestly, I don't know all the details of what he'd done or what eventually happened to him. Of course, forgiveness should not be rushed or forced. But I do know this. That night matured me. I grew a little bit more that night. It was hard, but maybe it's supposed to be hard.

Let me admit this, though. Sometimes, church is too hard. Dysfunctional, abusive churches exist, and I'm not suggesting anyone endures harm. A difference exists between something being harmful and hard. We should protect each other from harm while encouraging each other to persevere through hardship for the sake of growth. The former tears us apart, while the latter builds us up.

For years at my current congregation, two older couples led the way, Bill and Fran as well as Buford and Dot. They led us with grace, mercy, and maturity. When I think of the fruit of the spirit in Galatians 5 ("love, joy, peace, forbearance, kindness, goodness, faithfulness, gentleness and self-control"), I realize how fully I saw that fruit in them. Honestly, I've known many people who modeled this list in part, but few who demonstrated it as consistently and completely as them. When hard conversations arose, their patience always exceeded my own. When conflict came up, their peace always amazed me. When difficult people walked in the door, their gentleness overwhelmed me. When I gazed into their personal lives (marriage, family, career, etc.), all I saw was faithfulness. How did they do this? How did they end up like this? I've thought about that a lot, and I've come to this conclusion. They practiced a lot. The Holy Spirit had years to do its work. God worked through prayer, fasting, Scripture reading, and other spiritual practices. Among these, they practiced church involvement.

Each of these families helped lead our church for over fifty years. In that time, they saw huge attendance swings. They experienced times of growth and times of decline that brought about the occasional conversation of "Will our congregation survive?" They invested in the neighborhood, from local schoolchildren to the nursing home across the street. They supported missionaries who planted churches in multiple continents in the world. They heard church members complain and argue as well as unite and come together. They watched friends leave for bigger, fancier churches in the suburbs, and they welcomed the poor and homeless who ventured in on Sundays. They celebrated births and weddings as well as supporting one another through sickness and death. Through it all, they vacuumed, swept, held babies, changed light bulbs, cleaned toilets, and balanced budgets. I'm not sure how all of that sounds to you, but I can tell you this. If you commit yourself to this for five decades, you will grow to be more like Jesus. They endured the challenge of church participation and leadership, and they came out on the other side with great character, as Paul alluded to in Romans 5.

Was it hard? Absolutely. Maybe that was the point. Maybe it's supposed to be hard. The point of church is not to be easy. The point of church is to help us grow into the image of Christ. The church is not an end in itself but a means to an end—becoming like Christ. This is a huge part of salvation, and the church offers it in Christ.

I love church camp. I always have. Most every single summer of my life, I've gone away for a week out into nature with a church. Out in God's creation alongside sisters and brothers in Christ, I experience the presence of God. I play a lot. I laugh a lot. I grow in my faith. However, every single time, something bad happens. When people come together in close quarters for a week, getting little sleep in unfamiliar beds, they get cranky. Eventually, conflict arises. Someone crosses someone. Disagreement ensues. This has happened in every single camp week of my life. But every time, when the division comes, we work towards unity. We pursue reconciliation. It's annoying that it happens, but I go home stronger and more mature because of it. It's not a hardship to avoid but an opportunity to grow. When I grow and see others grow as well, I realize again the true worth of church.

The year of the Sonic tater tot blow-up, the same thing happened. Tempers flared. Accusations were thrown. Solid disciples cracked and acted less than Jesus. But, we sat down together. We talked openly. People listened to each other. People apologized to one another. I wouldn't say everyone felt great about it by the end, but everyone agreed to move on together. I wish it hadn't happened, but we left stronger because of it.

Why is church so hard? Because the goal is hard. If you see church as a destination for happiness, you'll eventually be disappointed. If you see church as training ground for spiritual formation, you'll have ample opportunity to work out, get stronger, and become more like Jesus. Expect that church will be hard. It's not a challenge to avoid but an opportunity to embrace. That posture will prove crucial for thriving in church.

19

A Place to Thrive

ON APRIL 15, 2019, the world watched in horror as the Notre Dame Cathedral in Paris burned for fifteen hours. The cathedral had been under renovation, and the fire proved accidental. Since construction began in the twelfth century and finished in the fourteenth, this beacon of Gothic-style architecture has long been a symbol of Parisian beauty. It serves as an essential part of what makes Paris a destination. Thankfully, the fire did not collapse or even completely destroy the cathedral. Within days, billions of dollars in donations from all over the world flooded into the reconstruction effort.[1]

Why did this strike such a nerve? After all, like America, Europe has experienced declines in church participation. Why did so many around the world pledge to rebuild the cathedral? I believe most of us have some good memories of faith and church. Call it nostalgia. Call it respect for tradition. Call it spiritual but not religious. Whatever label we want to give it, many hold a space in their heart for church. There's a sense in which, even if we're away from her, we miss her. We want to see her thrive.

Whether we admit it or not, we want to see the church at its best. We want to see the church beautiful. Deep down, we've had an experience of her beauty. We've gotten lost in the mystery of the sacraments. We've felt a moving of the Spirit. We've seen unconditional love face to face. We've spent time with people who really knew us. We've discovered a purpose and a sense that our lives really matter to someone bigger and beyond us. She ushered us into

1. Cuddy and Boelpaep, "Notre-Dame Fire."

all of this long before we experienced her brokenness. Now, we long to see her beautiful again. Like Notre Dame, we want to see her rebuilt.

The church lives in a cycle of decline and rebirth, apostasy and revival, crucifixion and resurrection. Much of American Christianity wallows in a hypocritical decline, but not all of it. Beyond America and Europe, in parts of Africa and Asia, signs rise of rebirth and revival. The question, for all of us, is this: What role will we play in the rebuild? Will we contribute to the brokenness or the beauty? Or, will we stand on the sidelines in a perpetual stance of deconstruction?

Friends, your pain is real. Your reasons for leaving are not without legitimacy. But if you've gotten this far, you may be wondering what it's like to give her another chance. What would it be like to participate not out of guilt or social convention, but out of a thirst for the kingdom? What would it look like to be part of the reconstruction? No matter your context, here are the steps to thriving in a church. It's easy to show up at a service a few times a year. It's a much different thing to thrive, to come alive in the body of Christ. As I've watched friends thrive in their return, three things prove crucial.

First, you need to deal with the past. As I've watched people come back to church, I've seen a common theme. Those who thrive are those who dealt with their pain and found healing. I think of my buddy Dan. Years ago, in his early to mid-twenties, he went through a season of heavy church participation. Over time, the hypocrisy from other leaders wore him down. Eventually, he grew weary that the church seemed more focused on looking good than doing good. Dan left that congregation, and for eight to ten years he stayed on the periphery of church, sitting in the back of a worship service a handful of times a year. When he and his wife began to have kids, he began to remember the beauty, and he wanted that for them. Still, the brokenness kept coming back to him. So, he dealt with it. Dan wrote it down. He saw a counselor, as well as a spiritual director. He honestly shared with his family of origin and close lifelong friends. Dan took his time. He got mad and angry. Over time, healing came, and he felt ready to reenter.

I think of one of the courses I teach at Lipscomb University. As part of our exploration of the Bible, theology, and church practice, I offer an assignment where students visit three different types of churches. As I packed up after class one day, one student hung around to chat. She expressed grave reservations about the assignment. Because of her past painful experiences with church, she couldn't imagine setting foot in a church building again. I listened. I told her I was sorry. I didn't want her to do anything she wasn't ready for, yet I encouraged her to write about her thoughts and experiences. Sharing our past with a trusted friend or counselor, as well as journaling, proves helpful. If we don't deal with our past, we'll experience paralysis in our future.

For the first couple of years after my mother's death, I didn't like to talk about her. I didn't like to look at her picture. I grew uncomfortable when people wanted to tell me stories about her. I just wanted to move on and leave that past pain behind me. A few years after her death, my dad remarried an amazing woman who became my stepmother, or second mom. Several months after they got married, I came home from school to an unsettling surprise. On the desk in my room, my second mom had framed a picture of my first mom. It made me sad, and my twelve-year-old self wanted to run from all of that. I went to her. "Why did you do this? It makes me feel sad." She put her hand on my shoulder, and I remember her saying, "I know it hurts, but if you choose not to remember, you'll miss out on all of the good memories. Just give it a try. Give it some time." For the first week or so, I couldn't see anything in my room but that picture. It hurt. Then, I gradually began to appreciate it. Stories about my mom came back. Old memories of the good times resurfaced. Years later, as I write this, that same picture in the same frame sits on my desk. If I hadn't processed the past hurt, I would have missed out on this future.

There's a biblical category for this—lament. Like the theme of exile, laments show up as one of the most neglected parts of the Bible. My favorite passages of lament include Psalms 13 and 22, along with Lamentations itself. The laments of the Bible ask vulnerable, honest questions about suffering and abandonment, even as they profess faith when complete understanding doesn't come. God is a big God. The Creator can handle our frustration. When you cry out the words of David in Psalm 22:1, "My God, my God, why have you forsaken me?," God listens. When we express the vulnerability of our pain only to realize it doesn't scare God off, healing begins. Take your time and name the hurt.

Begin the process of forgiveness, which Jesus taught and modeled. At his most painful moment on the cross, he extended forgiveness to others, even those who took his life. You may not be ready to forgive those in the church who hurt you, but I pray you can begin the process. I get nervous about rushing forgiveness, and I am convinced it often takes time. My friends Jerry and Dana experienced this. When their daughter went through significant challenges during her teen years, some at the church responded with unfair judgments. The sting of that made church really hard, and it took them close to a decade to come back. They had to clear the air and gently confront several people who had hurt them. Those were difficult, heavy conversations. Healing was not quick or easy. The path of forgiveness certainly provides complications and mysteries. I haven't completely figured it out, especially when it comes to deep darkness. But I know this. We should be open to the process of forgiveness even if the outcome remains unclear. After you have addressed your past experiences with church, faith, and religion, you are ready for the second step, picking a church.

How do you pick a church? I am convinced we often look for the wrong things. We pick in a way that often reveals a penchant for consumption instead of participation. If the latter is the goal, and I think it should be, then our selection will more closely resemble the following.

A few years before he passed, Krista Tippet interviewed Eugene Peterson for her show *On Being*.[2] Peterson pastored a church in Maryland for roughly thirty years, but he's most known for his books, especially his translation of the Bible, known as *The Message*. In his retirement, he returned to his childhood home in Montana, not too far from Glacier National Park. This segment shaped my thinking.

> *Ms. Tippett*: Exactly. I mean, your life and your writing is passionately interwoven with this enterprise, this aspiration of church.
>
> *Mr. Peterson*: That's true. We go to a small church. When I was a pastor of a congregation, people would leave and say, "How do I pick a church?"
>
> *Ms. Tippett*: Yeah.
>
> *Mr. Peterson*: And my usual question, my usual answer was go to the closest church where you live, and the smallest. And if after six months it's just not working, go to the next smallest. [*laughs*]
>
> *Ms. Tippett*: [*laughs*] OK, so what is it about small rather than big?
>
> *Mr. Peterson*: Because you have to deal with people as they are. And you've got to learn how to love them when they're not loveable. And we go to a church now that's—I'm a Presbyterian, but it's a Lutheran church. And most of the people are my age. And our pastor is young. And he's a really good pastor. But I don't go to church—I mean, I go there to be immersed in what I don't know about. And these people. I mean, there's 80 people in church, and I don't—I know some of them quite well. I grew up with many of them. I would just—they still treat me like a little kid.

2. Tippet, "Eugene Peterson."

Ms. Tippett: [*laughs*]

Mr. Peterson: And, so that's kind of refreshing.

I share this not out of a preference for small churches, although many thrive in them. I offer it up because it differs from the normal ways we choose churches. Peterson doesn't look for a church experience to consume but a people to do life with. He doesn't look for a church to go to but a church with which to thrive. When looking for a church, consider this list.

First, do you see beauty in their common life together? Don't fixate on programs, activities, and worship services. Focus more on how they live together. Notice the ways they love God, each other, their neighbors, and even their enemies. Look for the vibrancy of the unique things found in church—open weekly gatherings, intergenerational community, transnational identity, and ethical transformation. See the ways they provide social capital to one another. Resist the urge to judge the church solely by the music and preaching. Do not get caught up in branding and technology.

Second, does this church offer potential for thickness? Do you see a pathway into forming thick culture? Plainly, if you live far away, thickness will prove challenging. I think of my friend Justin. After he and his wife began living in the neighborhood where our church meets, they began walking to our gatherings. One day, I asked him why they'd chosen us. I expected to hear a compliment about our atmosphere or programs, maybe even my preaching. Justin just smiled and said, "It was the closest one to the house." Physical proximity often plays a role in potential for thickness. Moreover, if you have a life situation with which this church seems ill-equipped to blend, consider going elsewhere. For example, I think of my friends who have special needs. If the church does not have means for access or seems unwilling to provide it, look elsewhere. Look at the personality of the church. Are these the type of people you respect and with whom you could see yourself growing close? Think about your life rhythms and schedule as compared to the rhythm and schedule of the church.

Third, does this church demonstrate vulnerability and authenticity? Every church will manifest brokenness at some point. It lurks as part of the human condition. The key is this: Is the church willing to admit it? Are they a group of people eager to express vulnerability through the hard work of confession and repentance? Some churches harbor deep secrets and seek to protect the brand and history of the church name. You can measure a church's authenticity by the way they talk about themselves. Do they admit mistakes? Do they laugh at themselves? Do they pursue a professional polish or a humble simplicity?

Fourth, does this church offer a healthy theological fit? As I have said, I believe the Bible matters. I firmly believe in the God of creation, the divinity and humanity of Jesus, the reality of the resurrection of Christ, the power of the Spirit, and the inspiration of the Scriptures. More than that, I have deep convictions about various -isms that would bore you within a few paragraphs. These things matter, yet I am convinced that the most important thing is for people to come together in search of Jesus and in relationship for one another. Like anyone else, I would like more people to agree with me on all the intricacies of theology and all the issues of our day. But more than that, I want to see more gather around Christ. I believe if we gather, Jesus will ultimately take care of the rest.

With that said, you have to decide what theological issues are negotiable and nonnegotiable for you. In my congregation, when I have taught on this, I bring a Jenga tower with three colors—blue, green, and purple. The blue forms the bottom, the green the middle, and the purple the top layer. In Matthew 23:23, Jesus, when referring to the Old Testament, said that some commandments were weightier than others. Jesus gave us a greatest command and a second commandment that provide a foundation. The beliefs I mentioned above, like the nature of Jesus, these are the blue bottom layer for me. Things like my understanding of morality and ethics, as well as teachings on prayer and mercy, form the middle green level. But on that top purple level I place issues of preference, such as worship style or ministry emphasis. I try not to get too worked up about that top level. After all, if some of it falls off, the tower still stands. But if you start pulling out the bottom blue layer, it may all fall apart. You will have to do the hard work of labeling your Jenga tower. Exercise discernment. Don't put everything on the bottom foundational level. It's not only inconsistent with church history, but it's impractical. You'll never find that church. It doesn't exist.

After dealing with your past and picking a church, a crucial third step remains, thriving with your new community. How can you thrive in your new church? Invest. Make a long-term commitment to sacrificially invest in that group of people. No matter how good the church seems going in, be certain of this. They will disappoint you. Commitment prepares us to last through those initial letdowns. In the interview, Peterson recommends giving it at least six months. I encourage people, after a good selection process, to at least give it a year. However, it's crucial what you do in that year. You must dive in and participate to truly know if it's a long-term fit. After a year, if it's going well, commit in your mind to being there at least ten years. It's far too common, in our transient culture, to change churches every couple of years. While there may be cause for this at times, I believe it's far healthier for our spiritual maturity to plant deeper roots. The most mature Christians I know, by and large, have been at their current church for years.

Years ago, while helping out with an event at my college, I found myself chauffeuring an influential Christian leader. About the age of fifty at the time, he was a sought-after speaker and teacher. I asked him what advice he had for someone wanting to go into ministry. I'll never forget what he said. "When you go to a church, act like you're going to stay there for the rest of your life. You might not. In fact, you probably won't. But, act like you will. Commit your heart and mind to her. Because if you do, it will shape how you invest." Let that soak in. The rest of your life. That sounds intense, but when we make that type of relational investment, something truly powerful happens.

At a key moment, I made a long-term commitment to a relationship that felt awkward and even difficult at times. That relationship forever altered my life. In March of 1989, near my eleventh birthday, I met my two future stepbrothers for the first time, ages nine and five. My dad and future second mom took the four of us, including my biological brother, age thirteen, to Gatlinburg, Tennessee for the weekend. We crammed into a four-door sedan and set off on a road trip. There were ups and downs. I loved the idea of a big family, and at times it seemed like we all fit together perfectly. At other times, it seemed forced and awkward. The three of them had very different traditions and ways of doing things. In my frustration, I sometimes wondered, "Who are these people?" I'm sure they felt the same way.

Eleven months later, we officially became a family. For anyone who has ever been a part of a blended family, you know the challenges. It was hard, but in my heart I made a commitment. We all did. I will treat her like a mother even though she's not my biological mother. I will treat my two stepbrothers like real brothers even though we're not blood related. I leaned into a future that only existed in my hopes. And thirty-one years later, I can tell you this. They are family. The investment, on all our parts, made the difference.

But we had to sacrifice. All of us had to give up some preferences. We had to share rooms, and I even shared a bed for many years. We had to compromise on how to do traditions. We had to let go of a lot of frustrations.

If you had asked each of us to write down our dream of a perfect family, the reality we live in now differs from all our dreams. Yet, I discovered this. I can only speak for myself, but the reality actually turned out better than I hoped. I learned that real family, in all its complicated messiness, beats perfect imaginary family every time.

The most meaningful relationships of my life have been those that involved some level of sacrifice, especially those that involved mutual sacrifice. Sacrificing for others includes giving up getting our way and controlling the outcome. This includes our vision and dream for what that relationship, family, or church should be. Thinking of Bonhoeffer once again, you have to ask yourself, "What is it I really love—my dream of what this community could be or the actual people themselves?" That's hard, for I have a definite vision of what I want the church to be. But the church will never be what I want her to be. In fact, that's a good thing, for she's not my church. Jesus tells us that there is no greater love than laying down one's life for one's friends. That sounds noble and inspiring, yet we struggle to lay down our preferences, expectations, and dreams for others.

This all leads to perhaps a humbling and surprising conclusion. Thriving in a church isn't mainly about the church. It's more about you. It's more about me. Can I deal with past pain? Can I make a wise selection based less on what I desire and more on what makes a good healthy family? Can I make a long-term commitment to sacrifice my dream of community out of a love for real people? If you can do this, you'll thrive in a church.

Religious deconstruction is easy. Reconstruction of the church demands sacrifice. Throughout the cycles of church history, we've seen this. Francis of Assisi lived in Italy during the late twelfth and early thirteenth centuries. Growing up in great wealth, he eventually gave it all up to live in solidarity with the poor and outcast. He sought spiritual enlightenment and wisdom from God. However, he lived in a time of great hypocrisy. Many church leaders lived broken lives, and cynicism reigned. One day, near the old chapel of San Damiano outside of Assisi, Francis is said to have spoken these words. "Lord, what do you want me to do? Show me what you want me to do with my life." And the Lord answered. A voice as clear as the day responded: "Francis, go and rebuild my church, which, as you see, is falling down." At first, Francis took this in literal fashion. He sought money to begin a reconstruction campaign of this old church building. Eventually, the truth set in. God had bigger plans than that old building. The church is not a building but a people, a movement. Jesus sought the revival and restoration of his bride. Therefore, Francis began a religious order, now known as the Franciscan order, which sought to simply follow the teachings of Jesus. You might think of it as a reconstruction project, because they believed she was worth rebuilding.

Over eight hundred years later, people still mourn at the sight of a broken-down church. People still find inspiration at the thought of seeing her reconstructed. We long for that type of thing. We want to see the beauty of the church rebuilt. At some point, we've caught a glimpse of her beauty. Things haven't gone as planned, but we've never forgotten what that felt like.

You can have that again. You can shelter in her beauty once more. She's ready to welcome you. I want you to know that you can thrive in a church. By the power of the Spirit, let's rebuild her together.

20

Behold Your Mother

On that August Saturday night in Alabama back in 1986, surrounded by my brother, uncle, and grandparents, a hospital chaplain told me my mother had died. In a childhood instinct of self-protection, I cried out, "Who will be my mother?" My grandmother threw her arms around me. My grandfather gently put his hand on my shoulder. The chaplain comforted me and did his job the best he could. Eventually, we left the hospital and went to a local motel.

The next part of this story may not seem true. If you believe it at all, it may not seem loving. I've thought about it many times. I can assure you it's true, and I've discerned it as loving. Still, it's hard. Decide for yourself, I suppose. The next morning, my grandparents woke us up and took us to a local church. None of us had ever been there before. I assume they found it in the Yellow Pages. I never liked visiting churches. I loved my home congregation, but it always felt awkward as a kid to go to a new place. Imagine the awkwardness of this scenario.

Hours after my mother died, my grandparents took me to an old, nondescript church building. The building had wooden paneling and carpet popular in the 1970s. I remember a hundred or so folks dressed up in their Sunday best, each with a Bible under their arm. I felt especially self-conscious due to the large scab on my forehead, residue from the broken windshield the night before. It all felt like a fog, a bad dream. I was still processing what all had happened. We sat near the back. My grandfather went and found one of their leaders. He told them our situation. At one point in the service, the preacher, with a soft, earnest voice, shared our tragedy with the congregation. Nice strangers looked at me with eyes of sympathy. They bowed their heads and prayed for us. To an eight-year-old boy, it was all very uncomfortable.

For years, I never thought much about that morning. Since it was my experience, I considered it normal. Surely, everyone goes to church every Sunday, even if their mother has just died beside them hours prior. In my teen years, I finally realized the abnormality of that Sunday morning. Few would have woken up their grandkids and taken them to a strange church in a strange town. Why did Granny and Gramps do this so long ago?

I've wrestled with that question. For years, I didn't know how to ask. Eventually, that question went to the grave with them. Why did they do it? Perhaps their commitment to doing the right thing according to the rules at all times took over in the hazy grief of that weekend. Maybe this was it. It was Sunday, and good Christians went to church on Sunday. Maybe it was all about religious ritual.

I doubt it though. I think there was something more. I don't think Granny and Gramps took us there out of a guilt-ridden sense of religious obligation. I think it was something much more serious. I don't think they went for us at all. I think they went for themselves. Consider it this way. What makes a grieving parent get out of a motel bed in a strange town and venture into a strange church? Desperation. I'm convinced desperation drove us there that morning. Faced with the loss of their daughter and their motherless grandsons, they simply didn't know what to do. They were lost, so they went to the people where they felt found. When their family became broken, they reached out to their larger family, the church. I believe they experienced comfort among that little old church that morning. Amidst overwhelming tragedy and chaos, I believe that strange church family brought them a sense of grounding and stability.

It's all very messy, but sometimes I imagine it this way. I imagine they were trying to answer my desperate question with an equally desperate act. Who is my mother? The church. The church, wherever you find her, is your mother. Do I think all of that crossed their mind that morning? No. But is it consistent with how they lived? Absolutely.

More than what they did, though, it reminds me of something Jesus did which I've long sought to understand. On the cross, Jesus famously offered up seven sayings spanning the four Gospel accounts. Some demonstrate his grace. In Luke 23:34, "Father forgive them for they do not know what they are doing." Some invite us into mystery. In Matthew 27:46, "My

God My God why have you forsaken me?" Some give us the hope of heaven. In Luke 23:43, "Today you will be with me in paradise." In comparison to these, many overlook the following one.

In John 19:26–27, Jesus looks out from the cross to see his grieving mother and his close friend John. Both grieve the torture and ensuing death of Jesus, yet Jesus unselfishly thinks of them. To his mom, he says, "Woman behold your son." To his friend, he says, "Behold your mother." Mary was about to lose her oldest son. John was about to lose his best friend. Maybe you've been there in some way. That weekend in Alabama was my first but not only time. Life is fragile. Bad things happen. People die. What do we do when people die? What do we do when the "crosses" of this life come? How do we keep going? Who do we turn to when we lose those we've depended on?

Near the climax of the cross, Jesus did what he did best. He created. He created family out of a context of pain and loss. Before his own resurrection, he resurrected the losses of Mary and John. Mary did not so much lose a son on the cross as gain a son. John did not so much lose a friend on the cross as gain a mother. As they gathered around the cross, Jesus made them a family.

It still works the same way. When we gather around the cross, we become family. Jesus makes us a community. He makes us one. Because of this, we are never alone. If I've learned anything in life, this is it—church is my family.

Because of the tragedy in my childhood, I've always been resistant to putting total dependence on any one person or small group of people. After all, I learned firsthand that you can lose somebody at any time. However, I've never fallen for the lie of rugged individualism and total self-dependence. I've always sensed I'm hardwired for community. I need people. I've always craved a big family and lots of friends. My mother may die. My father may die. My brothers may die. My wife may die. My kids may die. Of course, all of that would be devasting. But, I would not be alone. Because if you have a church, you always have a family. Nothing can ever take that family away from you.

Every Sunday, I gather with people around the cross. Our worship culminates with the Lord's Supper. As I meditate on the cross, I bring all my wounds and brokenness to the Lord. Nothing is hidden. All is laid bare. On more than one occasion, my mind wanders back to that Labor Day weekend in 1986. I bring that valley of desperation to the cross. I take my great question to Jesus. "Who will be my mother?" I sit there in silence at the foot of the cross. And I hear him say what he said to John so long ago. "Behold your mother." His words offer no trace of sentimentality or naïve idealism. His words are true and credible with a proven track record of over three decades.

If I've learned anything in life, this is it. The church is my mother, and she's been a good mother to me. She hasn't been perfect, but she's been good. Has she been your mother? Has she been a good mother? If she hasn't been the perfect mom, ask yourself this. Does she deserve one more chance?

Every Sunday, I gather with my family around the table of the Lord. At a certain point, someone will hold up the bread and say, "The body of Christ, broken for you." In these times, I look around. I look around at the family around me, my broken but beautiful family. Are they annoying at times? Yes. Do they let me down at times? Yes. I annoy them and let them down as well. We haven't been perfect. Yet, I love them. I love them for what Jesus has done in and through them.

I look around at them. I see their faces. I see Ryan. Earlier this year, a tree fell on my house. Ryan drove right over with his chainsaw and spent hours cutting it up for me. I see Judy, who served for years as a nurse. The night before the doctor induced Beth to give birth to our second daughter, nerves got the best of me. I talked to Judy, and she lovingly calmed me down. I see Doug, a fidgety elementary school kid. He makes faces and gives me a thumbs up as I preach. I see Sara, a drama therapist who has as much energy as the rest of our church combined. A few years back, she convinced a bunch of us to do a "Thriller" dance at the church talent show. Let's just say that my werewolf moves need work. This is my family. These are my moms and dads, brothers and sisters, sons and daughters. I have a big family. I am not alone. My family is not perfect, but they're my family. So I keep going back.

At times, she's let me down, but I went back. Have you thought about leaving? Have you left? What might it look like to give her another chance?

Years ago, I asked the question, "Who is my mother?" In John 14:18, Jesus told the apostles that he wouldn't leave them as orphans. He kept that promise to me by giving me a church, fueled by the Spirit. I don't ever want my kids to have to ask the question. I don't want them to wonder. So, at times, I get a tad more serious than maybe I should for their age. Sometimes, I say this on a walk. Sometimes, I say this as I tuck them into bed. "I love you. I'm so thankful to be your dad. I want you to know something, though. I won't be around forever. Someday, I will die, and it will be sad. But you will not be alone. The church will be your family. The church will take care of you. No matter what happens, know this. Wherever you go in this world, if you feel alone, find a building with a cross. Walk in on a Sunday and eat the body of Jesus with them. This is your family. You will never be alone." Normally, they groan. "Daddy, why do you get so serious?" So, I smile and give them a hug. But deep down, I know they've heard me.

If I've learned anything in life, this is it. The church is my mother, and she's been a good mother to me. She can be a good mother for you. She may be broken, but she's beautiful. It may be hard at times, but she's worth it. Still worth it.

Bibliography

Barna Group. "Meet Those Who 'Love Jesus but Not the Church.'" https://www.barna.com/research/meet-love-jesus-not-church/.

Bethke, Jefferson. "Why I Hate Religion, but Love Jesus." Video of spoken-word performance. https://www.youtube.com/watch?v=1IAhDGYlpqY.

Black, Amy E. *Beyond Left and Right: Helping Christians Make Sense of American Politics.* Grand Rapids: Baker, 2008.

Bonhoeffer, Dietrich. *Life Together.* Translated by John W. Doberstein. New York: Harper & Row, 1954.

Brooks, David. "How to Fight the Man." *New York Times,* February 3, 2012. https://www.nytimes.com/2012/02/03/opinion/brooks-how-to-fight-the-man.html.

Cacioppo, John T., and William Patrick. *Loneliness: Human Nature and the Need for Social Connection.* New York: Norton, 2008.

Center for Spirituality, Theology, and Health, Duke University. "Welcome." https://spiritualityandhealth.duke.edu/.

Chatterjee, Rhitu. "Americans Are a Lonely Lot, and Young People May Bear the Heaviest Burden." NPR, May 1, 2018. https://www.npr.org/sections/health-shots/2018/05/01/606588504/americans-are-a-lonely-lot-and-young-people-bear-the-heaviest-burden.

Cuddy, Alice. and Bruno Boelpaep. "Notre-Dame Fire: Has Too Much Money Been Given to Rebuilt It?" BBC, April 25, 2019. https://www.bbc.com/news/world-europe-48039770.

Ferngren, Gary. *Medicine and Healthcare in Early Christianity.* Baltimore: Johns Hopkins University Press, 2009.

Friend, Tad. "Jumpers: The Fatal Grandeur of the Golden Gate Bridge." *The New Yorker,* October 6, 2003. https://www.newyorker.com/magazine/2003/10/13/jumpers.

Gladwell, Malcolm. *Outliers: The Story of Success.* New York: Little, Brown, 2008.

Gruber, "Religious Market Structure, Religious Participation, and Outcomes: Is Religions Good for You?" NBER Working Paper 11377. National Bureau of Economic Research, May 2005. https://www.nber.org/papers/w11377.

The Halo Project. "Halo Calculator." https://www.haloproject.ca/calculator/.

Henderson, Tim. "More Americans Living Alone Census Says." *Washington Post,* September 28, 2014. https://www.washingtonpost.com/politics/more-americans-living-alone-census-says/2014/09/28/67e1d02e-473a-11e4-b72e-d60a9229cc10_story.html.

Bibliography

Jones, Jeffrey M. "U.S. Church Membership Down Sharply in Past Two Decades." Gallup, News, April 18, 2019. https://news.gallup.com/poll/248837/church-membership-down-sharply-past-two-decades.aspx.

Khullar, Dhruv. "How Social Isolation Is Killing Us." *New York Times*, December 22, 2016. https://www.nytimes.com/2016/12/22/upshot/how-social-isolation-is-killing-us.html.

Mcgregor, Jena. "Ex-Surgeon General Laments 'Loneliness Epidemic.'" *Mercury News*, October 6, 2017. https://www.mercurynews.com/2017/10/06/ex-surgeon-general-laments-loneliness-epidemic/.

Olds, Jacqueline, and Richard S. Schwartz. *The Lonely American: Drifting Apart in the Twenty-First Century*. Boston: Beacon, 2009.

"One Thing You'll Find in the Obits of Many Long-Living People." *Eurekalert!*, June 13, 2018. https://www.eurekalert.org/pub_releases/2018-06/osu-oty060818.php.

Partners for Sacred Spaces. "Economic Halo Effect." https://sacredplaces.org/info/publications/halo-studies/.

Peterson, Jordan. *12 Rules for Life: An Antidote to Chaos*. Toronto: Random House, 2018.

Putnam, Robert D. *Bowling Alone: The Collapse and Revival of American Community*. New York: Simon & Schuster, 2000.

Roberts, Sam. "John Cacioppo, Who Studied Effects of Loneliness, Is Dead at 66." *New York Times*, March 26, 2018. https://www.nytimes.com/2018/03/26/obituaries/john-cacioppo-who-studied-effects-of-loneliness-is-dead-at-66.html.

Saad, Lydia. "Catholics' Church Attendance Resumes Downward Slide." Gallup, News, April 9, 2018. https://news.gallup.com/poll/232226/church-attendance-among-catholics-resumes-downward-slide.aspx.

Solzhenitsyn, Alexander. *The Gulag Archipelago*. Translated by Thomas P. Whitney. New York: Harper & Row, 1974.

Steinbeck, Joseph. *East of Eden*. New York: Viking, 1952.

Sunde, Joseph. "The Halo Effect: The Economic Value of the Local Church." Acton Institute, July 20, 2016. https://blog.acton.org/archives/88116-the-halo-effect-the-economic-value-of-the-local-church.html.

Thomas, Gary. *Sacred Marriage: What If God Designed Marriage to Make Us Holy More Than to Make Us Happy?*. Grand Rapids: Zondervan, 2001.

Tippet, Krista. "Eugene Peterson: The Bible, Poetry, and Active Imagination." *On Being* (podcast), aired December 22, 2016. https://onbeing.org/programs/eugene-peterson-the-bible-poetry-and-active-imagination-aug2018/.

The Unlonely Project. "Not by My Selfie." The Foundation for Art & Healing. https://artandhealing.org/unlonely-overview/.

Vedantam, Shankar. "Guys, We Have a Problem: How American Masculinity Creates Lonely Men." Transcript. *Hidden Brain* (podcast), NPR, March 19, 2018. https://www.npr.org/templates/transcript/transcript.php?storyId=594719471.

Willard, Dallas. *The Divine Conspiracy: Rediscovering Our Hidden Life in God*. San Francisco: HarperCollins, 1998.

Made in United States
Orlando, FL
12 December 2021

11595210R00104